# *Stories of the Outback*

Published by Brolga Publishing Pty Ltd
ABN 46 063 962 443
PO Box 12544, A'Beckett St, VIC, 8006, Australia
email: markzocchi@brolgapublishing.com.au


First printed 2007.

National Library of Australia Cataloguing-in-Publication data

Bolton, Bert (Richard Albert), 1923- .
Stories of the outback.
ISBN 9781921221736 (pbk.).
1. Bolton, Bert (Richard Albert), 1923- .
2. Executives - Arnhem Land (N.T.) - Biography.
3. Tourism - Arnhem Land (N.T.).
4. Aboriginal Australians - Arnhem Land (N.T.).
5. Wilderness areas - Arnhem Land (N.T.).
I. Title.
338.4791092

Printed in Indonesia
Cover by David Khan
Cover photograph by Barrie Bolton
Typeset by Diana Evans

# *Stories of the Outback*

*Bert Bolton*

# *Dedication*

This book is dedicated to my loving wife Rona, for her encouragement, devotion and patience. I frequently made changes, adding or deleting pages of my stories after she had spent hours on her computer, printing and positioning pages, and correcting my atrocious spelling.

To our great friend Margot Vaughan for her wonderful drawings and paintings that illustrate my stories.

And my sincere thanks to Rolf Harris for his painting of me, as well as his inspiration and encouragement to me over many years, inparticular to write these stories.

# Contents

# *Preface*

The inspiration for me to tell outback stories began back in 1948. I was a trainee engine driver on the Commonwealth Railways, relieving on the Port Augusta–Alice Springs line. While waiting to work my next train south I often spent down time at the busy Oodnadatta railway depot. One day, Terry Agar the stationmaster and his wife Shirley invited me to dinner.

Two men at that dinner were outback icons, Reverend John Flynn and Arch McLean.

I had never met John Flynn although I was well aware of his dedicated work for the sick and needy in the outback. I knew him as "The Camel Man".

Archie McLean I knew by virtue of the fact I had often helped him load cattle he was sending to market on the trains. Archie was the manager of Peake cattle station.

During the evening Arch told us a wonderful story about the life of his boss Sidney Kidman, The Cattle

King, which I retell in this book.

That evening changed my life and ignited a passion of storytelling. From that night forward I began making notes and writing stories about all the outback pioneers and characters I came in contact with. Great old men and women such as Mort Conway, a grand old drover; Matt Wilson, Storekeeper/Publican at Timber Creek on the Victoria River; bush nurse Sister Ruth Heathcock of Booroloola; Mrs Christina Gordon of the old Vic & Don Hotels in Darwin.

The old man I'll always call my mate (first punch), Noel Healey of Dunmarra Hotel. Noel worked on the Pearling Luggers at Broome and on the Canning Stock route. Sadly he was murdered by bikie drunks in 1968. I won't forget my Aboriginal mates in Arnhem Land, Blanasi, Jungawunga, Tjoli Laiwonga, Gulpilil and old Mandarg.

During the early sixties I went with Len Tuite from Alice Springs to Ayers Rock (now Uluru). In 1967 I bought a tourist coach and started operating my OUT-BACK TRACK TOURS. Over the next 30 years I told those stories hundreds of times to my coach tour passengers. My friend Rolf Harris liked to listen to my stories and he gave me plenty of hints on delivery, articulation, and especially eye contact with an audience. I also learnt from listening to another great storyteller, the late Len Beadell. My story telling led me to working with some of the great entertainers of Australia, including Rolf Harris, Bobby Limb, Ted Egan, John Williamson and Jimmy Little.

In 1971 I was commissioned by Woolworths of Sydney to travel to Arnhem Land and organise a group of Aboriginal dancers to perform at the Waratah Festival in Sydney. I knew Arnhem Land well after many visits to that country – fishing and hunting with my young tribal friend, Blanasi. With his help I was able to gather together the best ten dancers in Arnhem Land along with himself, a great didgeridoo player. The ten dancers, a song man and Blanasi formed the group on arrival in Sydney.

Woolworths provided a semi-trailer as a stage and so the Aboriginal dancers along with the song man and didgeridoo player performed in full cultural dress, body paints and feathers. They mesmerised tens of thousands of people along the route. Later that day they danced at a concert in Hyde Park. As a result of the huge success of that visit to Sydney the group and I were invited to perform at many major events in the years to come.

Rolf asked me if I could arrange for Blanasi and his didgeridoo along with song man, Tjoli Laiwonga, to perform with him at the very first performance in the concert hall of the Sydney Opera House. This was another huge success.

A few months later I was asked by the Federal Government to produce the after-dinner entertainment for 3000 American and 2000 Australian travel agents on the occasion of the 41st ASTRA WORLD TRAVEL CONGRESS 1971. Again I brought the Aboriginal dancers to Sydney. The Americans and most of the Australians had never heard the music of a didgeridoo or seen tribal Aboriginals dancing their dreamtime stories. My part was to explain the story of each dance.

Because of the large number of guests the only venue large enough in Sydney at that time was Randwick Racecourse. Utilising the grandstand for the guests and the saddling paddock for the dancing, we lay a 10 x 10 metre sand square in the middle of the green grass paddock. On the two front corners of the square we had built piles of wood that were then splashed with petrol. The dancers, painted up in luminous traditional designs, were hidden in a large bark hut at the back of the sand square ready to enter the arena on a signal from me.

After dinner the guests filed into the grandstand to take their seats. On my signal the unique haunting sound of the didgeridoo began echoing out of the loudspeakers. The didgeridoo player was still out of sight in the bark hut. The large floodlights turned on illuminating the sand square. Suddenly two brilliantly painted men appeared from the bark hut and ran to the front of the sand square, sat down together and started to twirl a hard fire stick into a groove on a soft fire stick. Beneath the fire sticks had been placed two tufts of dry grass. The twirling action creates burning dust to fall onto the dry grass. Within 50 seconds both men jumped to their feet holding a flaming fist of grass. They ran to separate corners of the sand square and threw the flaming grass onto the petrol-splashed piles of wood which erupted into large fires. The roar from the 5000 amazed guests would have been heard on the other side of Sydney. Then the dancing began. This was my greatest show production.

We also performed in a number of Bobby Limb shows including the South Pacific Medical Convention at the Anthony Horden Pavilion in Sydney. The South Pacific Rotary Convention at the Exhibition Building in Melbourne, and The Southern Hemisphere Corn Growers Convention in Brisbane. In between these shows I would fly outback to join one of my coaches for a few days telling stories.

I always wondered why my passengers often said to me, "Bert, you are always on holidays".

Self portrait by Rolf Harris

# *Introduction by Rolf Harris*

I'm a bit hazy as to when Bert and I first met. I think it was in 1967 on a ferry in Darwin in the Northern Territory of Australia.

My wife Alwen and our daughter Bindi were returning to the UK and I was really keen to experience some didgeridoo playing first hand. To this end it had been arranged that we should visit the aboriginal settlement at Mandorah, a short boat ride from Darwin.

By some chance Bert was on that ferry, and introduced himself as a lifelong friend and tribal 'blood brother' of Blanasi, who had just recently been flown to London to appear on my television show, where he was a huge hit. Bert and I got on like a house on fire.

Fast forward, if you will, to the Sydney Opera House in 1973. I was to perform the first ever show in the

Concert Hall of that newly opened building, and I had arranged to have Blanasi and his long time friend Tjoli Laiwonga, dance man extraordinaire, on the show. I found out that Blanasi was staying with Bert at his Sydney home, and when I met up with Bert again at the rehearsal, he suggested we should 'go bush' with Blanasi, a couple of his aboriginal mates, and a friend of Bert's called Harry Ellis.

This trip eventually took place in 1974 and was a remarkable, life changing experience for me. We went right up through Arnhemland, and were almost marooned when we ran out of fuel in Maningrida. However, that's another story.

Back to Bert. I was exposed to his amazing story telling the next time we met. This was in 1989 I think, when I was filming a sequel to the first ever documentary filmed in Australia in colour. That was made by the ABC in 1969 and was called 'Rolf's Walkabout'. The sequel, 'Rolf's Walkabout, 20 years down the track', re-visited the places we'd been, to see the changes. We went to Bamyili where Blanasi lived, and he played didgeridoo to accompany me singing 'Sun Arise' as the sun lifted above the horizon. It was magic.

Bert was there, organising our travel arrangements and when we camped at Katherine, he regaled us with some riveting stories of the heroes of the Australian outback. I remember a bunch of tourists were attracted to our campfire to listen to Bert's stories of Harry Redford, (the model, I believe, for Captain Moonlight in Rolf Boldrewood's classic Australian story 'Robbery Under Arms'), Sir Sydney Kidman the cattle Baron, Daisy Bates, and many, many more. I watched these people from all walks of life, sitting round that campfire, mesmerised, as I was, by Bert's story telling. I said to him afterwards, "You must record these stories! You are absolutely marvellous, and these yarns you've told us tonight would make an amazing television series or an extraordinary book".

I'm so thrilled to see that Bert has finally done it and got these fascinating stories of this special area of our country and our history, into print. Enjoy.

*Rolf Harris*

# *Ernest Giles Expedition*

The leader of the expedition was sitting on a rock with his eyes transfixed on the vast desert wilderness to the west that was confronting his exploration party of four men.

On a high point of the remote Rawlinson Range he now had to make a life or death decision. Normally explorers in desert regions move forward from one range to the next. Ranges generally provide rock-hole catchments for water. From his vantage point no ranges could be seen, possibly for a hundred or more kilometres. Ernest Giles was no ordinary explorer, he would be right up there with the best Explorers of the Australian outback, such as Sturt, Gregory, McDouall-Stuart, Eyre, Forrest, Warburton and Leichhardt. Jumping to his feet with a last look at the formidable country ahead, he began scrambling over the rocks making his way down to the foot of the range. His favourite horse, the Fair Maid of Perth, was tied to a tree near the Circus Waterhole. Mounting his horse he shook the reins and urged her into a gallop, making his way back over the 32 kilometres to his base camp at Fort McKellar.

Giles marshalled his three companions, his second-in-command Harry Tietkens, Alf Gibson and James Andrews. "I have made my decision," he announced. "I am unable to ascertain if a range exists at a reasonable distance from the Circus Waterhole at the end of the range. I will take one man with me. We will endeavour to cross the sandhills for up to 160 kilometres to enable me to plan our next move."

Giles would have preferred to take his second-in-command Tietkens, instead of the less experienced and less intelligent Gibson, however, he decided Tietkens would be more capable of guarding their camp, spare horses, and food supplies in the event of an attack by the unfriendly natives they had encountered in the vicinity.

On 20th April, 1874 Giles and Gibson departed Fort McKellar. Giles riding the Fair Maid of Perth, Gibson riding a big strong bay horse and trailing behind two pack horses each carrying a 25 litre keg of water, their food supplies and a cooking pot. Their swags were strapped to the back of each rider. The two men camped overnight at the Circus Waterhole and set off early next morning. After travelling 16 kilometres, they crossed the dry bed of Lake Christopher and the first of the spinifex covered sand-hills. After travelling 32 kilometres Giles called a halt to rest the horses and have a meal of smoked horseflesh and a Johnny cake. Giles was distressed to find that Gibson had foolishly failed to pack a full supply of food and now they only had enough for one week instead of two. After another 32 kilometres they made camp for the night in very desolate country, with no suitable grass for the horses. The next day their travel saw a change of country, but not to any great advantage, flat gravelly plains, firm but not stony with some patches of spinifex. At the next rest stop Giles noted that one of the water bags had leaked some of their precious water. At that stop Gibson decided to switch to ride one of the packhorses instead of the big strong bay horse. Giles could not understand his reason for the change. The loss of water through the leaking bag worried Giles as he now believed there would not be enough water for the four horses. Consequently, he decided to give the two pack horses a drink and then turned them loose driving them along the track a short distance to make their own way back to the Circus waterhole and hopefully back to the good feed they knew at Fort McKellar. The remaining two horses were given a drink.

The two kegs were then tied up in a tree for their return journey. They then continued on for another 32 kilometres before making camp for the night. Through the night, the thirsty horses roamed near the camp and found one of the water bags tied up a tree and bit a hole in it, spilling all the water.

After travelling 128 kilometres the country was still flat and gravelly with occasional patches of spinifex but there was no sign of a range or even hills. The two men now only had a few litres of water in one canvas bag and no water for the horses until they arrived back at the kegs. The next day, when they were 170 kilometres from Fort McKellar, Giles could see a small line of ridges that could have been hills about 40 kilometres in the west-north-west direction. Giles was hopeful of reaching these ridges or hills with the chance of finding water. Gibson, however told Giles that his horse was travelling poorly and doubted it would make it that far. Not long after, Gibson's horse staggered and fell down dead.

With a sad heart Giles had no alternative but to retreat immediately. He perused the scene with his field glasses with the intention of returning to this position again soon. He then named the ridges Alfred and Marie Ranges after their Royal Highnesses the Duke and Duchess of Edinburgh. The Fair Maid of Perth was only too willing to retreat. Now she had the extra weight to carry with Gibson's saddle and swag. They continued retracing their tracks with one riding and one walking. When they were about 50 kilometres from the kegs Giles was walking and he called out to Gibson to halt until he caught up. In the meantime Giles had concluded in his mind that they could not continue with one walking and the other riding as they were travelling too slowly. They were both extremely thirsty and they had only a litre of water between them that they drank. Giles then said, "Look here, Gibson you can see that we are in a most terrible position with only one horse. One walking as one rides. I believe that in my condition I would not be able to walk back the 150 kilometres without food or water. In any case one must walk behind. I have decided that I will walk whilst you ride ahead and bring relief to me. Now Gibson you listen to me. You must ride ahead and cover the ground to the kegs by tonight to give the horse a drink. The mare will not last long if she does not get a drink soon. Let her rest for a while and then ride on. Early tomorrow you will sight the Rawlinson Ranges. Gibson, I rely on you to alert Mr Tietkens to bring me relief as soon as possible. I will endeavour to get along the track as far as possible." Gibson replied that he fully understood the instruction. Giles asked Gibson to leave as much water for him as possible when he reached the kegs.

Gibson replied, "Alright."

As Gibson rode away Giles called out one last instruction.

"Stick to the tracks and don't leave them until you

reach the Circus waterhole." Quickly, the Fair Maid of Perth carried Gibson out of sight.

Giles walked at a slower pace than when he was trying to keep up with the horse rider. The country was still gravel with large clumps of spinifex scattered along the way. Giles did not expect to reach the kegs until late the next day. After nightfall, Giles continued walking, following the horse tracks in the moonlight until the moon went down. He lay on the gravel but was unable to sleep. Not only was he incredibly thirsty and hungry he was tormented by little black ants that crawled over and bit him constantly. Also, he was conscious of the presence of poisonous scorpions in the desert. He worried that Gibson might ride past and miss the kegs in the dark in which case all would be doomed.

At daylight Giles continued to follow the horse tracks. He saw that Gibson had dismounted and tied his own saddle up a tree to lighten the load on the Fair Maid of Perth and to help the mare walk at a good rate. Giles reached the kegs about midday after walking 24 kilometres that morning. It was obvious Gibson had been at the keg, given the mare a good drink, and emptied one of the kegs and part of the other keg. He left Giles about 10 litres in one of the kegs. He had to control himself from drinking too much of the water as he realised it would be all he would get until he met the rescue party. If he didn't meet them he doubted he would be able to walk to the Circus Waterhole, 100 kilometres away without food or water. Giles searched the bags and all he could find to eat were eleven sticks of smoked horseflesh each weighing about 55 grams. He immediately ate two sticks raw, as he didn't have a container to boil the meat.

As Giles sat, resting, he knew the odds of him surviving were very slim. To make matters worse Gibson had not left any canvas bags to carry water: consequently he was forced to carry the water in the heavy keg.

To carry the keg with the water he was forced to pad his shoulder with a folded cloth and use a stick bound to the keg with the stick across his shoulder. Under this handicap he walked all day and most of the moonlight night. His walking now was much slower under the extra weight he was carrying. After he stopped to rest for the night he was disappointed to see by the notes he had made on the outward journey over this day and half a night he had only covered 8 kilometres from the kegs. Since he had waved goodbye to Gibson he had now walked 58 kilometres in daylight with temperatures near 38°C. By strict rationing of water and smoked horseflesh Giles staggered on for kilometres at a painfully slow pace.

Often he would fall to the ground in a daze and not know how long he had been on the ground or even what day it was. After the third day he had finished the horseflesh. The day temperature was still 38°C and he was still carrying the heavy keg with only a few mouthfuls of water left. At 25 kilometres from the kegs Giles saw that the two loose horses had left the tracks and headed in a south-east direction. He was horrified to see also that the foolish Gibson on the Fair Maid of Perth had followed the loose horses' tracks. Giles walked along the loose horse tracks following Gibson's tracks for several kilometres hoping that Gibson would realise his mistake and return to the correct tracks. Giles was forced to return to the other tracks because of his exhausted condition. He was always watching anxiously to see if Gibson's horse returned to the correct line of tracks. They never did.

Four days after leaving the kegs, Giles was still 30 kilometres from the Circus Waterhole and he had drunk all his water and eaten all the horseflesh. His thirst was agonising and choking him in the high temperatures. Only his indomitable spirit and great strength of character enabled him to keep fighting. The last 30 kilometres escaped the memory of Ernest Giles. He continued walking in a semi-conscious state. On reaching the Circus he crawled on his stomach to the water's edge and drank and drank for how long he did not know.

After recovering his senses he could see that Gibson had not been at the waterhole as there were no tracks. He then felt incredibly hungry. He was relieved to know that somehow he had reached the end of the Rawlinson Ranges, but still he was 32 kilometres from his base at Fort McKellar and safety. With his worn-out boots and sore feet he began staggering on towards Fort McKellar. Not long after he departed from the Circus Waterhole he disturbed a female wallaby which in its panic had thrown its joey (baby) out of its pouch. When Giles saw it he pounced on the baby wallaby like a lion and ate it alive. He never forgot the delicious taste of that animal.

Another very hot day forced Giles to rest in the shade of a large gum tree at the base of the range. He was again tormented by thirst. Late that day Giles arrived at a large freshwater lake, which he had named The Gorge of Tarns when he first set up the Fort. The lake and surrounding shores provided water for many ducks and other birds coming into drink. Numerous kangaroos and wallabies made handy food supplements for the explorers and there was plenty of good sweet grass for the horses. When night and cooler weather arrived Giles set out to cover the remaining 8 kilometres to Fort McKellar. He arrived at one in the morning. Imagine the enormous relief Ernest Giles felt as he limped into that base camp. He woke Tietkens in his tent. Tietkens was so shocked at the condition of his leader that he just sat up and stared as if he were someone from another planet. Giles was terribly upset and saddened when Tietkens told him that neither Gibson nor the loose horses had come back. Therefore, Giles was the only one of six living creatures to survive from that journey in the desert and the clutches of death.

Having come to the conclusion that by now Gibson

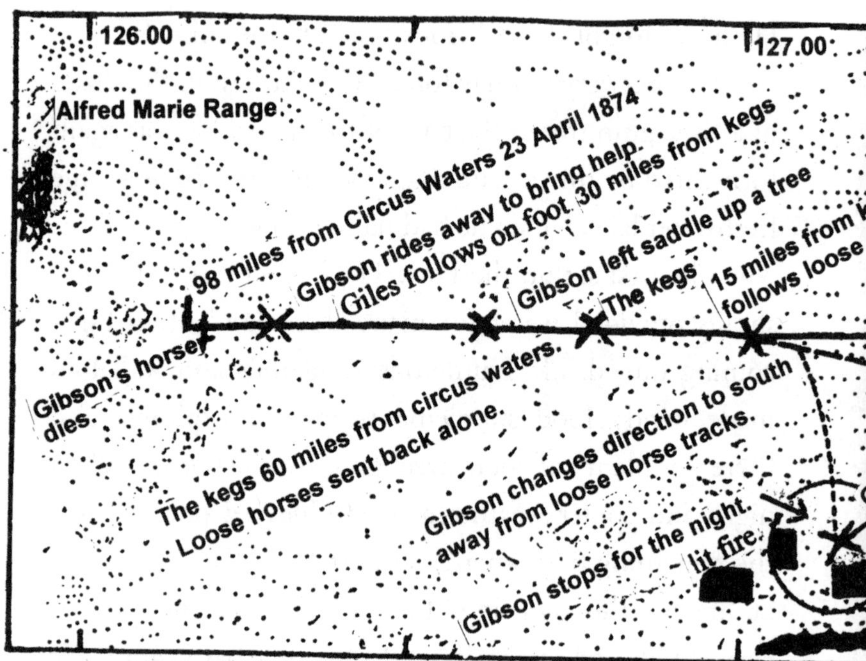


Bert Bolton and his Groups searched shaded areas in 1975 1980 1

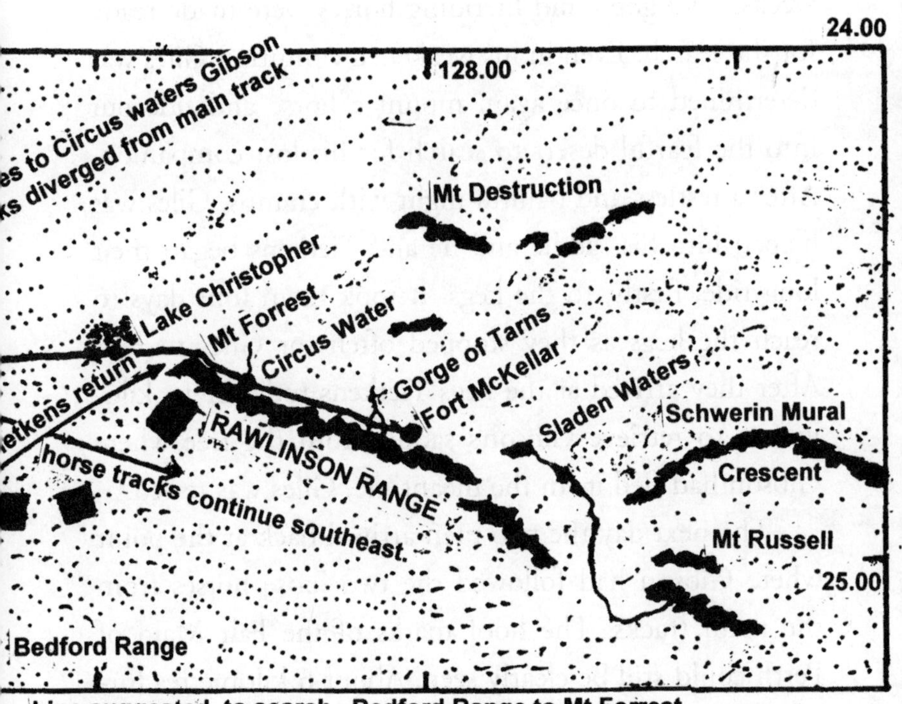


Line suggested to search. Bedford Range to Mt Forrest.

must be dead, Giles decided they must try to recover his body. Giles rested for the remainder of the day and night. Tietkens prepared the bags of water, and loaded them on to two packhorses. He packed enough food for two weeks. Two good and fit riding horses were made ready for the search. Even in his weakened condition Giles was determined to once again mount a horse and ride out into the fearful desert to search for his lost companion. After a restless and painful night with cramps, Giles was helped into his saddle and he and Tietkens began their long ride; firstly, to the kegs. It took them four days to reach the kegs as they stopped often for Giles to rest. After they arrived at the kegs Tietkens rode on 16 kilometres to retrieve Gibson's saddle from the tree where Gibson had tied it. In the meantime, Giles was rested.

The next day the two men arrived back at the point where Gibson had followed the two loose horses from the main tracks. The hoof marks of the Fair Maid of Perth could still be clearly seen. About 6 kilometres further on they saw where Gibson had veered away off the tracks of the two loose horses.

He was now heading directly south. As the tracks became harder to follow from high on a horse's back, the two men took it in turns to walk. This caused them to track Gibson much slower. Both Giles and Tietkens were mystified as to the reason Gibson stopped following the loose horses tracks, as they could still be seen clearly. It was suggested that Gibson might have thought the horses had veered to the north. He may have been trying to use Giles' compass that he had asked Giles for before they parted. Gibson had never before used a compass and it is most likely he had made a fatal mistake.

That night while they camped they lit a large fire and talked over their situation. Tomorrow, if they had not been successful with their search by midday, they would be forced to abandon as they had now been away from water for 4 nights. At that time Gibson was heading nearly due south. From high on the sand hills in that direction could be seen the small ironstone hills known as the Bedford Range. A few months before Giles and James Andrews had visited those hills seeking water.

The next day they found the Gorge of Tarns. If Gibson had mistaken them for the Rawlinson Range and made for them he certainly would not have found water in the Bedford Ranges. It could be that Gibson did in fact reach the Bedford Ranges. From there he would clearly see the Rawlinson Range and he may have changed direction once again. From that point to the Circus Waterhole would be over 100 kilometres and far beyond the capabilities of even the Fair Maid of Perth in the condition she was in at that time.

The mare had no water or food for a number of days. Somewhere in between the Bedford Ranges and the Rawlinson Ranges lay the remains of the Giles expedition, such as his saddle frame, stirrup irons, bridle irons, horse shoes, Giles' revolver and ammunition, and his treasured favourite Gregory patent compass. At midday the next day Giles and Tietkens set a course directly to the northern end of the Rawlinson Range more than 64 kilometres away. Before they arrived back at the Circus Waterhole they had crossed the tracks of the two loose horses still heading in the east-south-east direction – not in the direction of the ranges. On arrival at the Rawlinson Range Giles, honouring his fallen companion, said "I name this place the Gibson Desert."

***The following insert is from author, Bert Bolton:***

*In 1952 I was working out on the Nullarbor Plain in the town of Cook where I met Len Beadell. He was at the time engaged in the surveying of a site to become Maralinga, the operational centre for the Atomic bomb tests to be conducted by the British some time later.*

*Len and I often discussed the Giles expedition and in particular the fate of Alfred Gibson and the location of his remains. Where Gibson died is where the Giles equipment is lying waiting to be found.*

*One aspect we discussed was,* Could the equipment survive all this time without rusting and rotting away into the desert sands? *I explained to Len that on a number of my visits to the top end of the Nullarbor Plain where the Great Victoria Desert begins (that is where the sand-hills and scrub starts) I had a number of times come across pieces of leather harness, such as a leather bridle with steel mouth piece still attached to the leather. Also I had found parts of old cart wheels.*

*These objects would have been discarded back in the 1880s or thereabout when the old Afghan sandalwood collectors were working in the area. Consequently there is no reason to believe that out there in the mostly dry desert iron parts and leather would not remain today.*

*These talks with Len so long ago fired my imagination of the Giles expeditions.*

*Len told me a few years later, that he was surveying the route for his Gunbarrel Highway when he realised he was in the Gibson Desert area where Gibson died. Consequently he spent a couple of hours driving around in his old Land Rover looking for any sign of the Giles equipment without success. As the years rolled by in the early sixties I started my company OUTBACK TRACK TOURS, which I operated for thirty-five years.*

*Eventually my tour routes grew, covering more than half a million kilometres all over the Australian outback. One of my requirements when arranging a new tour was to take a four-wheel drive vehicle over the proposed route to check the track's suitability for a large coach to travel on. The planned new tour was to travel from Alice Springs via Ayers Rock across the Gibson Desert to Laverton in Western*

*Australia. At last after all those years as a Giles fanatic, I was in his country. From that trip I became a student of everything Giles. From my experience now of the area I am convinced the equipment can be found. People not familiar with the area do not agree. They say drifting sands would cover it. My answer to that is that the sand-hills are mostly stable with very little movement, caused by wind. Clumps of spinifex assist to make the sand-hills stable.*

*Years later I met Len Beadell once more and he reaffirmed his belief that the equipment would be buried deep below the sand. I told him that I thought it was thirty-five years since he built the Gunbarrel Highway through that area. He agreed. I asked him how come the sand hadn't covered all the sardine tins, bully beef tins, tobacco tins and even bottle tops he left around his campsites along the track between the Rawlinson Ranges and Warburton. He left his trademark by the way he always set up the rocks around his campfire. Even today that is still my argument. Over the last thirty-one years I have organised and operated three major search expeditions into the area, in 1975, 1980 and 1987. Each included 40 people working from our nearby base camp. At the selected area to be searched all the walkers would line up 10-15 metres apart and walk about 12 kilometres. After stopping for a rest and lunch, the group would then move to the right or left and walk back to the starting point. Over the years I have had many dedicated searchers helping me. Probably the most enthusiastic helper I had was the late John Bechervaise. John used to be our navigator. He had great experience with a compass from his days as the leader of the Australian National Antarctic Research Expedition.*

*Now I'm too old to do any more exploring but I am sure that one day somebody will take up the search started so long ago by Ernest Giles and Harry Tietkens, then continued on by Len Beadell and my self in the '70s and '80s. The one thing I'm sorry about is we didn't have vehicles with land-mine detectors fitted in case spinifex had grown over the equipment. My very good wishes to any future search.*

The three men spent the next week preparing to abandon Fort McKellar and begin their long return journey back to civilisation. They shot another spare horse and smoked the flesh, repaired some of their equipment, shod their horses, and relaxed a little by swimming in the lake.

On the 3rd May 1874 the return journey began. Giles mapped a course along the northern side of the Rawlinson Range. To his advantage, now he knew where the water lay ahead along the familiar route. Travelling via the ranges and waters he had previously named Sladen Waters, Schwerin Mural Crescent, the Petermann Ranges, and the mystic dome shaped Olgas (now known as Kata Tjuta). Finally on the 9th June they were comfortably camped in the shade of magnificent melaleuca trees next to a clear rock waterhole at Ayers Rock (now known as Uluru). The horses were well catered for with fresh green grass.

During this relaxing time Giles contemplated his achievements so far on this expedition. He agonised over his failure to execute his plan to be the first explorer to cross Australia. He did not need to consult his journals to remember his previous failure. However history has shown that his first and second expeditions had not necessarily been failures. He had mapped new lands, even if they were not the productive fields of grass that the financial backer wished for. Giles now set his return course. He was reluctant to follow explorer Gosse's track north. Instead, he wanted to blaze a new track directly east to the Overland Telegraph line.

After five days rest Giles moved his group on. He had mapped a route east. He expected to locate water at Mt Connor. No water was found in that region, so without replenishing his water supplies he continued east into the confused and difficult sand-hills. This eventually forced him to retreat back to Ayers Rock. As there was no alternative Giles was forced to swallow his pride and follow Gosse's track along a narrow neck of land over Lake Amadeus, to the George Gill Range, the Palmer River, back to Peake and finally Adelaide.

The first expedition had largely been financed by Giles himself, with some finance and encouragement from Baron Von Mueller, the well-known botanist who had accompanied A.C. Gregory on his Northern Australia expedition in 1855. The group on Giles's first expedition had consisted of only four men because of the shortage of finance. Even so, Samuel Carmichael offered to pay his own expenses in order to join the expedition.

On returning to Adelaide from his second expedition Giles was not welcomed with a great deal of fanfair, such as the welcome given to Edward John Eyre, Charles Sturt and John MacDouall-Stuart before him. Even the native Western Australian John Forrest was hailed as a hero. The treatment of Giles was probably due to the fact that on this expedition his achievements did not appear to be spectacular. However Giles did map and report on thousands of square kilometres of unexplored country in Central Australia.

The third Giles expedition funded by Thomas Elder with assistance from Baron Von Mueller was mainly of an exploratory nature. His main purpose was to seek information and conditions such as water availability on the route chosen for Giles' main push to cross Australia between 29º and 30º parallels west of longitude 127º. Giles was very familiar with longitude 126º and 127º as it was the place of poor Gibson's demise. Giles started his third expedition from near Fowlers Bay in South Australia. He gathered his group at Yatala Station, and departing from his usual practice he now included camels along with horses. He had already advised Thomas Elder that he would take camels on his fourth expedition to Western Australia. Firstly he travelled across the Nullarbor Plain following the Telegraph line to Eucla West Australia, returning by the same route to Fowlers Bay to restock supplies. His next objective was to determine the usability of the water-soak at a place the Aborigines called Youldeh (Daisy Bates called it Ooldea).

Giles believed he had discovered the extent north of the Nullarbor Plains. He then made his return via Finniss Springs Station on the Overland Telegraph Line, then down to Thomas Elder's Beltana Station. At the conclusion of his third expedition Giles had proven his selection of camels instead of horses to be correct for the expedition to Perth on his fourth expedition. On his third expedition every horse he took died of thirst whilst the camels proved their reliability in the dry waterless country. A huge advantage in favour of camels in the outback is that camels thrive on the leaves of shrubs and small trees. Horses need grass that is scarce in most places in the dry outback. The third of Giles' expeditions was made no less interesting by the fact that as usual he gambled with many of his decisions and unwittingly placed his team members in grave danger. However, if that is a fault of Ernest Giles it also is one of his strengths. Those sorts of decisions led to much of his success as an explorer. It could be said that some of the risky decisions he made on his third expedition were because he was aware it was eating into the time of departure for his fourth expedition to cross the country to Perth. Some of his gambles came off simply by luck. For example, he departed Wynbring Water to travel 400 kilometres across to Finniss Springs station without any knowledge of possible water in the country. On the eighth day after leaving Wynbring all their water was gone, their horses were dead. The only thing in their favour was the camels were still travelling well. At this point they were in such a desperate position that they were incapable of searching for water. Certainly they could not have survived another dry night. Only luck could save them. With two hours of daylight left, a small glint of reflection caught Giles' eye through a clump of mulga trees. There, leading to a dry salt lake, was good quality fresh water trapped in a small channel.

That stroke of luck saved the exhausted explorers and allowed them to continue on their journey to Finniss Springs Station, which they reached four days later. They travelled down the made track to Thomas Elder's Beltana Station, to end Giles' third expedition.

By the 6th May Giles was ready to fulfil his long-awaited ambition to cross the continent to Perth in Western Australia.

Mr Phillipson, the manager of Thomas Elder's Beltana Station, had done a particularly efficient job of organising some of the men for the workforce of the expedition. Giles had communicated frequently with Thomas Elder, requesting certain people as his choice. Elder conceded to Giles' requests. He wrote to Tietkens offering him the Second in Command position, which Tietkens gladly accepted.

Phillipson was meticulous in his selection of camels, some especially for riding and others for pack carriers. Phillipson for a number of years had been experimenting with the use of bullock camels (castrated camels) for carriers and they had proved to be better than bull camels for that task. Bull camels are sometimes hard to manage, particularly if there are female camels in the team.

When Giles arrived at Beltana Station at the end of April, Phillipson had everything ready for the departure of the expedition: packsaddles, bulk provisions, cooking equipment, canvas water bags, rifles, ammunition, tents, along with 22 specially selected camels – two of them bullocks. Some of the provisions were in storage at Port Augusta which meant that Giles and his crew had to take a leisurely journey of 240 kilometres over 10 days to retrieve them. This allowed Giles time to iron out any problems that could occur with a newly formed team.

The team of eight men included Ernest Giles as leader; Harry Tietkens, second in command; Saleh Mohamed, Afghan camel man; Alex Ross, young drover; Jess Young, newly arrived Englishman; with Peter

Nicholls, Tommy Oldham, and Jimmy, an old Aboriginal, from the third expedition.

The journey to Port Augusta proved useful practice for Giles in management of the biggest team he had ever had on an expedition.

On this short journey he clashed several times with Afghan Mohamed over his unacceptable treatment of some of the camels.

On departing Port Augusta, Giles set a course north along the western side of Lake Torrens. He then turned west to Wynbring Rock Waterhole. Further west, on arrival at Youldeh (Ooldea) soak, he once again established a depot. Tietkens and Jimmy, who was returning home after the third expedition, were dispatched with four camels to be delivered to Fowler Bay on orders from Thomas Elder. The party now numbered 7 men and 18 camels.

The time at Youldeh was spent repairing gear and making canvas water bags and other work equipment. In the meantime Tietkens and Tommy were exploring the country ahead for water. They discovered water 146 kilometres ahead. The group travelled this in short sections taking 5 days for the 146 kilometres to Ooldabinna. To extend the water supply they dug wells. This allowed them to stay longer at this location so Tietkins and Tommy could go ahead and search for water once again. However the wells failed to produce enough water. Giles was forced to once again take a risk with the hope of finding water ahead. The camels were loaded with enough water for approximately five or six days. After 224 kilometres, sufficient water was found, and good small scrub for the camels to eat.

As they advanced further they saw tracks of kangaroos and emus, along with other animal tracks. With Tommy's knowledge and bushcraft he showed them the flight of pigeons that again led to water. The water was not plentiful but provided enough for several days. This waterhole was dug by Aborigines in the bed of Lake Serpentine near the Western Australian and South Australian border and was named Boundary Dam.

At Boundary Dam camp the camel men got somewhat careless, not shortening the camel's hobbles, which meant that they then could walk much faster than if they were short-hobbled. There was great danger to Giles and his men when they failed in the morning to find the camels. They survived only because of the fitness of young Alex Ross, who was tracking the camels at a fast rate. He caught them and returned to camp hours later to find a very worried Ernest Giles and his men. If Alex Ross had not caught the camels when he did, the whole group would surely have perished.

As Giles and his group started to pack to leave Boundary Dam, not knowing what was before them, *hey presto!* It started to rain and continued for several days.

Giles caught water in canvas sheets and was able to fill all his waterbags. The group continued westward, once again travelling in dry country with things again looking serious with no sign of water. Giles had organised the main group to travel straight ahead whilst Tommy and Tietkens travelled on a path several kilometres on each side of the group. Suddenly they saw Tommy galloping and yelling excitedly, "Water! Water!". He had by chance caught site of a large pool of water – Queen Victoria Springs.

Another day and another Giles gamble. The nearest likely water was Mount Churchman at least 520 kilometres ahead. Once again Giles found several rock holes with sufficient water at short distances apart to allow the group to continue on and reach a good waterhole in amongst rocks. This waterhole was called Ularring. Giles decided to rest up and relax and give the camels a break as there was plenty of food for them in the vicinity for several days. Little did he know what was in store for his party. Several very friendly natives approached the camp, and mingled in a friendly manner. One of the natives was a girl of about 10 years of age along with several boys of similar age. The girl was really enjoying herself, walking among the men and examining the tents. Five or six adults sat on rocks nearby taking in all the strange objects the uninvited guests that had arrived in their camp. As evening approached the men were eating their meal when suddenly all hell broke loose.

A hundred or so natives encircled the camp at a distance of 100 metres and on command began yelling and throwing spears. The men scrambled for their guns and began firing over the heads of the natives. Several natives at close quarters got birdshot pellets in their legs and backsides. One large native charged at Giles from behind one of the tents and grasped him with two hands around the throat. Giles, in defence, brought his knee forcefully into the native's groin. He immediately released his grip on Giles's throat and joined his brothers in retreat into the bushes. This sudden attack was unprovoked and quite unexpected. Giles was now forced to mount an all night guard.

Rather than risk another attack Giles decided to move on the next day. Once again he was gambling on finding water. Two days later they came across another good water-rock hole they called Pigeon Rock Hole.

After departing Pigeon they encountered very thick scrub that took its toll with serious cuts to the camels' legs and bodies. The men who were walking also had great difficulty with the scrub.

On arrival at Mount Churchman they found more water to satisfy their needs. Not long after they departed Mt Churchman they came to their first outstation and met a white man. That night they all enjoyed a roast mutton dinner, after many weeks on short rations it was an unexpected delight.

Nearing the end of their journey, they had lost only two camels. The final 150 kilometres was enjoyable as they travelled on made roads and were greeted all along the way by people waving and cheering the four explorers.

The weary but happy group arrived on the 12th November at the Benedictine Monastery of New Norcia, which is approximately 120 kilometres from Perth. Giles decided to stay a few days at New Norcia to rest and clean up before the proud four explorers acknowledged their welcome to Perth.

Giles led his gallant men into the main street of Perth to the cheers of hundreds of people. Giles had now achieved one part of his ambition. The second part was to return across Australia along the 24th parallel.

The triumph of Giles and his companions continued in Perth for two months. In that time they attended a number of banquets and listened to many congratulatory speeches.

The start of the return journey began with another departing ceremony and an escort from many of Perth's dignitaries, led by Western Australian hero – explorer John Forrest. The only regret and sadness Giles felt on departing Perth was the fact that he had lost two of his officers. Mr Tietkens was returning to Melbourne by ship, stating he had personal business to attend to, and

Mr Young, the Englishman, was returning by ship to Adelaide to explore other offers to advance his career in Australia.

Giles now had a team of five. Himself; Alex Ross, whom he appointed second in command; Saleh Mohamed; Tommy Oldham; and Peter Nichols. Giles did not consider engaging replacements for the departed two. Thus he bestowed extra duties on the four remaining men. This meant Giles would have to abandon his usual practice of looking for water in dry country, having two men riding out on each side of the advancing main group. The method had saved the explorers at the Queen Victoria Springs, when Tommy was an outrider and had found the water that would have been missed by the main group.

The first section of their return journey was to Geraldton 480 kilometres north of Perth. With many stops and stays it took some weeks to arrive at the very pleasant town. Giles had a good excuse to stay even longer at Geraldton. He was waiting the arrival of a mail-carrying ship from England.

The explorers departed the western seaboard to head northeast. Their last bottle of champagne was cracked open at Pia Springs Cheongsam Station with the last white men they would see for many weeks.

After leaving Cheongsam Station they were uncomfortable with the close attention they were experiencing from a group of Aborigines. They did not make contact but followed at a distance for several days until the explorers passed Mount Gould. Continuing north, Giles established a depot on the Ashburton River. He explored as far north as the Ophthalmia Ranges before returning to the depot.

The exploration of the country now became serious as Giles set his course due east. Above his selected course were the tracks of Warburton. Below were the tracks of Forrest.

Giles started directly east to the Rawlinson Ranges, 960 kilometres away through unexplored country. For Giles this was his last throw of the dice to satisfy his pastoralist backers by finding new productive land.

From Giles' previous experience in this area he knew there would be no turning back. To his advantage on this occasion he had eleven fit camels to carry water and supplies. After struggling for 480 kilometres they found a native well they named Deep Well. Some of the crew discussed the folly of continuing on this course, but the confidence of Giles encouraged them to continue. Concern was felt after travelling 370 kilometres from Deep Well when they stumbled on a small channel with a useful amount of water available that provided some immediate relief.

The country now reminded Giles of the desert country he knew so well in the Rawlinson Range region. One thing in the travellers' favour was the pleasant weather with cool days and even colder nights.

However Alex Ross' camel Buzoe was beginning to be a concern and was acting extremely distressed, only walking very slowly and holding up progress. Giles at one point thought of shooting Buzoe, even though she was one of his favourite animals. The next morning, however, that drastic action was not necessary, as Buzoe was found dead. A stone memorial was built for her among the dry outback ground.

The name Buzoe's Grave is on the map in honour of poor old Buzoe. Just four days later a low ridge appeared on the horizon. In the mid afternoon Giles called a halt, the group had arrived at ground which was familiar to Mr Giles and Mr Tietkens, although all the other men knew what to expect because of the stories told to them.

As was the practice at night camps, Giles, seated on his small folding chair in the shade, would engage himself by entering into his log book the days events. Date; Travel time; Distance; Longitude 125°70' Latitude 24°10'; Time of Sunset 5:38pm. Young Alex Ross was designated at this time to erect Giles' tent and arrange his bedding. All hands have their various duties when making camp. But today was different. Giles sat surveying the scene with his field glasses. This camp was at the northern end of the Alfred and Marie Range which are Ironstone hills. Certainly no water would be found here, Giles thought, as he perused the scene before him.

Giles sat thinking, *What if? What if Gibson's horse hadn't died when it did?* He and Gibson would have found themselves here at the Alfred and Marie Range that night. *What if Gibson's horse had died here?* Most likely all would have perished here.

Looking through his field glasses, he imagined he could see the clump of Desert Oak trees where the horse had died a little over two years ago. Giles could not concentrate on his logbook entries. His eyes kept wandering back to the scene before him. After the evening meal Giles was soon off to bed. His mind was going over events of his disastrous second expedition. At last, sleep came to the troubled Ernest Giles. He muttered loudly in his sleep. Other members of the party camped nearby were woken by the strange and unusual behaviour of their leader.

The listeners could clearly hear him call out. *"Gibson, stick to the horse tracks and don't leave them until you get to the Circus Waterhole. Gibson, stick to the horse tracks. Stick to the tracks."*

*Oh yes, and another thing from Bert Bolton. Each time we mounted a search in the Gibson Desert we always invited a couple of local Aboriginals from the region to join our group. On the 1980 expedition an old tribal man, Wally Border from near Giles Weather Station, and his tribal mate, Ivor*

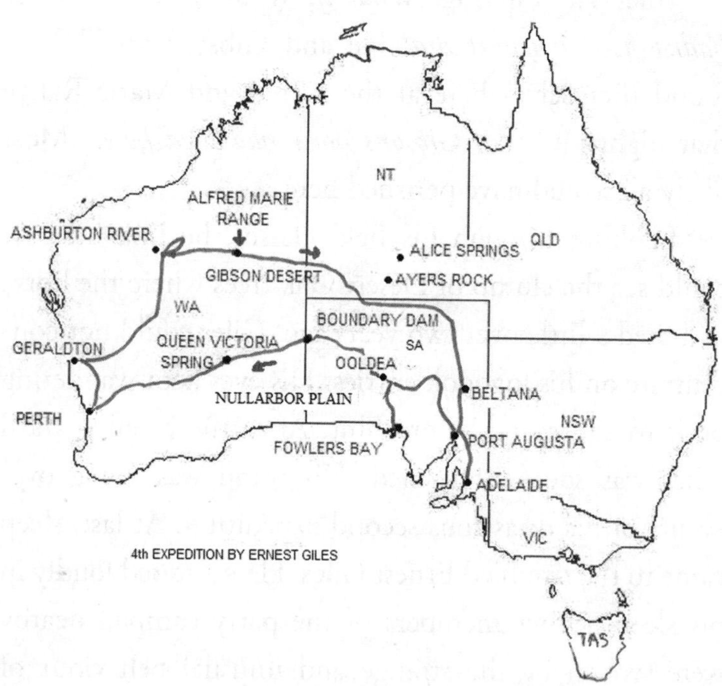


*Sheppard of Docker River, came along with us.*

*One evening the two Aboriginals and my mates John Bechervaise, Harry Ellis and I were sitting near the camp-fire yarning about old times. Wally Border told us that his real tribal country, where he was born was directly north at Turner Hills near Lake MacDonald. We listened with interest to his story of his childhood in that remote area years ago, about 1925. Harry asked, "Wally, when did you first learn that there were white people in the world?"*

*His reply had the three of us listening in amazement. "When I was about 6 or 7 years old, my Grandfather told me that when he was a young boy his father had been in a fight with four white men who came into their country riding large animals that the Aboriginals had never seen before. The white men shot and killed several tribal men. They were then speared to death that same night. The large animals were also speared and eaten." John, Harry and I just sat dumbfounded.*

*John said, "That would have been about 1849 or 1850."*

*Harry said, "What ever happened to Leichhardt?"*

*We both looked at John.*

*"That is a good question," John replied. "Over the years there have been a number of theories Some unreasonable, such as, Leichhardt's party getting caught in a flash flood in the Cooper Creek. Another was that he followed the rivers to the Gulf and set out to the Swan River via Roper River. If he took that route he was surely lost. We know at the start he headed for the junction of the Barcoo and Cooper Creek. His most likely route from there would be north-west across the Diamantina and Mulligan Rivers, passing the top end of the Simpson Desert (no problems at that latitude). Field and Hay creeks have good waterholes in good seasons, and it is good country then to the MacDonnell Ranges. Continue to Haast Bluff, sit on a rock like Giles did and look west. Four or five days later they would be at Lake MacDonald."*

*That just may be so.*

# *Flynn of the Outback, the Camel-man*

Jim McGinty had spent fifty years of his life in the outback, mostly in the remote regions of Birdsville, Cordillo Downs, Innamincka and Marree. He was a windmill and artesian bore mechanic and he had always worked alone.

In 1921 he was working on an artesian bore 30 miles east of Clifton Hills Station near the big red sandhill on the Birdsville Track. Without warning he was struck down with an attack of malaria, a disease he had never before experienced. He felt dizzy, so he lay down in the only shade available under his cart. He believed he would recover shortly.

In fact, he fell unconscious and was near death. He opened his eyes to stare into the friendly face of a young man bending over him wiping the sweat from his face.

Jim McGinty had heard of the Camel-man but had never met him. On this occasion by a stroke of luck or providence the Reverend John Flynn had arrived at the artesian bore to water his camels and to camp the night.

On seeing the unconscious man lying in the shade under the cart he immediately recognised the symptoms. From his meagre kit of medical supplies he took out quinine and administered the drug to the unconscious man. He sat nearby and anxiously watched as the man stirred and eventually opened his eyes. The friendly face had a broad grin. "Well well, old man, the next time you decide to leave us you must leave a note." There and then a friendship was formed of more than 30 years.

It was the time of the solstice, December days in Central Australia are extremely hot. The gales of the solstice blow huge clouds of dust across the country. A dust cloud can rise up to 3000 metres and travel hundreds of kilometres. Dust clouds that originate in Central Australia have darkened the skies in New Zealand 4800 kilometres away.

On this day the dust was so thick the young Camel-man closed his eyes and left the direction of travel to his friend Sudah, the camel. Trailing behind Sudah were three pack camels joined by a long cord connected to each of their nose pegs. At times the Camel-man had to hold onto his saddle horn when gusts of wind formed giant willy-willys swirling and twisting and spiralling high above the ground.

With the slow gait and rhythmical motion of each step the Camel-man swayed back and forth as he dreamed the day away. Each step reduced the distance he had to travel to his final destination, with only 1600 kilometres to go.

The Camel-man was a dreamer. His mission in life was to help others. His dream was to help bring comfort to the people of very remote regions of Outback Australia. To achieve this he had to learn of their most urgent needs, both medically and spiritually. He had to go and meet these families. This constant travel cost money. He did not have that sort of money.

To assist, his sister wrote a letter to the local newspaper suggesting the community in the small Victorian country town could help to raise money for his project. Gradually hundreds of people became interested and willingly contributed to the fund. By 1911, $400 had been raised.

John Flynn was born in 1880 in the small Victorian country town of Moliagul and ordained in the Presbyterian Church in 1910. He later joined the Smith-of-Dunesk Mission as a minister in South Australia. With the finance raised he was sent on a 4800 kilometre journey of investigation, through central Australia, the

Northern Territory and western Queensland.

Day after day the Camel-man rode on. Hours melted into days, days into weeks, and weeks into months. As he rode he dreamt of the day he would bring medical aid to families living in remote regions. Their needs were communication, transport and hospitals. His dreams were extremely unlikely to come true.

An eagle glided overhead. Both the Camel-man and Sudah the bird until it disappeared over a hill. Wouldn't it be wonderful if humans could fly, thought the Camel-man. He hoped those clever men Lawrence Hargrave of Sydney and the Wright brothers in America would be successful in getting their aeroplane to fly. As afternoon merged into evening, two white cockatoos flew over the Camel-man and with his bush knowledge he changed direction. Those cockatoos were pointing the way to a nearby waterhole that should be a good place to camp for the night.

As he approached the waterhole, two large red kangaroos hopped away slowly from the water's edge and then stopped a short distance away and sat back on their tails with ears pricked, watching the camels. On the other side of the waterhole two emus walked away with slow strides then also stopped to watch the intruders. Suddenly, with a loud whirr, a thousand budgerigars flew up from the water's edge and away in ever-increasing circles.

The camels lurched down forward, then backward and down forward again to finally settle kneeling on the ground with a rumbling grunt. The Camel-man stepped onto solid earth and stretched his long limbs. He was a strongly built young man with a pleasing thoughtful face. His blue eyes were the eyes of a dreamer. From the water bag he took a long drink, then carried his two-quart pots to the water's edge to fill.

Then he turned his attention to his hard-working camels. He was always kind to what he called his friends. He unloaded their pack carriers and led them to water. After he short-hobbled them he turned them out for the night to graze on the leaves of the shrubs nearby. Gathering some dry grass and dead sticks, he built and started a welcome fire. By the reflections of the fire he mixed his dough in a small dish, sifting it with fingers, next a dash of soda and baking powder. He poured in some of the cloudy water and mixed it with his fingers to form a firm dough. He punched and rolled with his clenched fist before breaking and flattening each portion into a cake between his palms. The quart pot had boiled and he made a mug of tea. Raking out the coals he placed the Johnny cakes on the hot coals.

His frugal meal included Johnny cakes with tinned corn beef washed down with black tea. After twelve hours in the saddle on a camel's back this was luxury indeed. After his meal he rebuilt the fire and spread out his swag. He then sat down and lovingly filled his straight-stemmed pipe and lit it with a burning stick. Matches were like gold in this country. Finally, laying back on his swag gazing above at the millions of stars, sleep came to the tired traveller.

The area he was required to service was about half the size of Europe. Stationed at Oodnadatta in lower central Australia, he travelled thousands of kilometres in all directions. He made friends easily and often made contact with lonely prospectors, railway gangers, bore sinkers and stockmen. Many of his duties included nursing sick children or mothers, sometimes hundreds of kilometres from medical or hospital facilities.

John Flynn had many sad stories to relate. One of many was the sad occasion when he advised the father of a young family struggling to establish a cattle station to seek medical treatment for a growth that appeared on the side of his head. This involved travelling with John Flynn for five days in a buggy to the nearest town, Marree, and then departing by train to hospital in Adelaide. On examination his tumour was too far advanced and the doctors could not operate. The man died that night. It was a long and lonely return to Marree and on to the little homestead where the mother and four young children were waiting for their father to return home. With heavy heart John Flynn had the very sad task of telling the children that Daddy would not be coming home.

John Flynn had worked in the field for Smith-of-Dunesk Mission for twelve years before he was in a position to put into action some of his dreams. The Smith-of-Dunesk Mission came into existence in Scotland many years ago. Its roots in Australia came from a young Scottish lad who perished in the Outback of Australia. His grieving mother, Mrs Smith of Dunesk, had bequeathed to the Free Church of Scotland certain sections of land the income from which was to be devoted to humanitarian work in the Outback of South Australia. After many years the accumulated rents and interest had provided additional capital of over $4000. The legacy that started the Smith-of-Dunesk Mission lay forgotten among papers of the church in Scotland for over forty years. It was Rev. F. W. Main in Adelaide, South Australia who one day examined an ancient Blue Book, raised his eyebrows and paused in thought. The bequeathed rent money was found to be correct.

On a rare visit to Sydney, Rev. John Ferguson, Chairman of the Board of Home Missions, interviewed John Flynn. The board immediately decided that the project of John Flynn should be presented to the General Assembly of Australia. Within three hours a meeting was convened and John Flynn's scheme was endorsed and the scheme was placed in the white book of the General Assembly of Australia.

Two hours later John Flynn started a twelve-month investigation and information-gathering tour across the

Outback of Australia. His travels would begin at Oodnadatta, visiting Sturt (Alice Springs) across the Tanami desert to Halls Creek in the Kimberley. Broome, Port Hedland, Wyndham and Katherine to eventually finish in Darwin. He travelled a total of 5263 kilometres. His mode of travel varied according to what was on offer along the way. To begin his journey he accepted a ride from a cattleman going to Sturt with his horse and buggy. The crossing of the Tanami desert was creating a problem until he met and was invited to accompany an Afghan camel-man and his team of 40 camels.

Mohamed Alibun had been crossing the desert with his camel-train, carrying supplies for the miners at Halls Creek and cattle stations in the West Kimberley, three times a year for a period of ten years. This journey took 60 days travelling at about 20 kilometres per day. Much of the travel time each day was reduced by the time it took each morning to round up the grazing camels and load them before departure, repeating that amount of time each evening unloading and turning them out for the night. Flynn admitted the work with the camel-team was tough going, however he was happy to do the work because the experience with the camels and the teachings of Mohamed would remain with him for the rest of his life.

The terrain of the Tanami interested Flynn; it was unlike a desert. Most of the country supported forests of desert oak and mulga trees (acacia). Near waterholes and floodplains huge termite mounds stood up to two metres tall around which grew Mitchell and Flinders grass and great ghost gum trees.

At the Granites goldfields, Mohamed gave his camels a days rest. During that stay John Flynn spent some time with two very lonely gold prospectors who had left their wives and families down in Victoria two years before. There had never been an opportunity to communicate with their families or the outside world in all that time. Flynn relayed all the world news he could remember, even though most of it was very old. For hours that night the two men sat writing letters to their families and other relations. In the morning they handed the letters to Flynn for posting when he arrived in Darwin. All mail dispatched from Darwin was transported by ship to southern ports.

At the Tanami goldfields several mines had been in production since the turn of the century. Around a campfire that night John Flynn heard the story of the courage of the Gordon family. Gold was first found there by Duncan Gordon in 1896. Gordon had been struggling to establish a cattle station that he called Bamboo Station, over in the northwest of Western Australia near Marble Bar. The cattle sale prices had been very poor and Gordon decided to leave his wife and three young children at the station whilst he ventured off to the Tanami region prospecting for gold. He was in a similar position in relation to contacting his family, as were the two prospectors Flynn had comforted at the Granites. When Gordon met a traveller passing through the Tanami who was going to Port Hedland on horseback, he gave him a letter to take to his wife Christine at Bamboo Station.

The note said:

*Christine, I have found good gold-bearing seams. Things are about to change for the better for our family and us. Pack up the spring cart, harness the horse, load the children aboard and come on over here.*

The enormity of the suggestion can only be considered when it is realised that the period was the 1890s. The distance was 1600 kilometres. Roads were almost non-existent, and the country was mostly unexplored. At that time wild natives still roamed the bush. This situation today would be very hard to comprehend, particularly as many people today are reluctant to move out into the streets at night in their city.

Christine Gordon and her three children arrived safely at the Tanami to join husband and father. Several years later the Gordon family moved to Darwin. There they leased the famous Victoria Hotel in Smith Street, and built the Don Hotel – two hotels that still stand today.

Slowly the line of camels plodded on, finally arriving at

Halls Creek. At every town and cattle station Flynn visited, he listened with interest to all the heroic stories that the proud locals relayed to him. An old prospector sitting on a box in front of his tin shack near the China Wall (a large quartz outcrop named by the locals) attracted the attention of John Flynn. With a friendly smile he said, "Hello old chap, it's a pretty warm day."

"Not hot today," the old chap replied. "It's only about 36ºC. Sometimes in February after the wet we get 44ºC. That'll fry an egg in your pocket."

"Well that may be so," replied John, "but I don't carry my eggs in my pocket."

Both men laughed. John took a seat on a nearby rock and the two men chatted away for over an hour as the old man reminisced about old times on the Halls Creek goldfields.

"Them was tough times. We all helped each other, mateship was very important. Did you ever hear of old Russian Jack, and what he done for his mate?" the old man asked.

"No, I haven't heard that one," replied Flynn.

"Well, it was way back in '89, Russian Jack and Tony the Pom come over from Pine Creek, been working together for years. They just settled in on the other side of the creek down there and they struck some good colour, but Tony got crook. He had a bad fever that looked like malaria. Plenty of miners around here were dying from it then. No medical facilities here in them days. So to save his mate, Russian Jack put him in his wheelbarrow and set off up the track to the nearest doctor at the hospital in Wyndham, 560 kilometres away. That's what mates did in them days," the old man said.

To continue his journey John Flynn travelled on the weekly mail truck down to Marble Bar and Port Hedland. At each town he called meetings and together with the the locals made plans for future nursing homes and hospitals. He retraced his route back to Halls Creek and on to Wyndham. This part of John's journey impressed him greatly. As a boy he had read the stories of the explorers Augustus Gregory and Alexander Forest. He had followed the travels of pioneers such as Patrick Durack and Willie McDonald. Between Halls Creek and Wyndham he marvelled at the majestic Carr Boyd ranges. The grandeur of the Kimberley Ranges is breathtaking. The picture of very ancient times is clearly evident throughout the region.

John Flynn spent a week at Wyndham where he lived at the hospital and took great pleasure in being entertained by the resident doctor and sisters who made up the hospital staff. He then followed the mighty Victoria River to the Depot at Timber Creek where he chatted to old Matt Wilson who showed him the tree Gregory had blazed at the time he was searching for Burke and Wills.

John Flynn enjoyed his short stay with the humorous

raconteur. Matt had operated the store at The Depot Timber Creek for over 50 years. Flynn loved to hear his stories of the history of the region dating back to the time of old Captain Joe Bradshaw – cattle station pioneer on the Victoria River. Captain Joe was the magistrate for that area. On official occasions he wore his old Sea Captains uniform. At the trial of cattle thief Jimmy Campbell, accused of stealing cattle from Victoria River Downs Station, Captain Joe sailed his small steamboat from his cattle station up the river to the Depot and set his court house up under the boab tree next to the bar room. His bench was an old beer carton. The case attracted stockmen and station owners from far and wide, not only to follow the proceedings of the trial, but also a rare occasion to meet their fellow pioneers. To open proceedings he drew his six gun and banged it on the old box announcing, "This court is open to hear the proceedings".

Matt Wilson rose to his feet and announced. "Your Honour, as it is such a hot morning may I suggest that first we should drink a toast to Queen Victoria." This was agreed. A toast was then offered for a fair trial by the accused Jimmy Campbell and seconded by the prosecutor Dickie Townsend. A toast was offered for the Wave Hill mob for their attendance. Another toast was proposed to the health and well being of Magistrate Captain Joe and many other toasts to relations and friends. Matt was very happy to encourage each toast suggestion. He had plenty of whisky and rum to sell. Finally Captain Joe again banged his revolver on the box and summoned the plaintiff and defendant to stand before him. The magistrate said in a stern voice "Mr Townsend and Mr Campbell, you are both pioneers of this harsh and remote country and you have both worked together for many years. I suggest that you two can settle this matter out of court." Both men agreed to a settlement. Captain Joe Bradshaw looking around at all the well bred horses tied to the trees, once again banged his gun on the box and announced. "This case is dismissed. I see some mighty good looking horses out there let's have a race meeting."

After a few days in Katherine, Flynn travelled the 112 kilometres down to the Maranboy tin mining fields, where he found an epidemic of malaria was causing great concern. Before departing, Flynn promised the miners he would emphasise in his report the urgency of their case for a hospital.

Finally he arrived in Darwin after twelve months of gruelling travel. Once he even had to walk 160 kilometres to get to his destination after a mail truck broke down. Now he sat down to recount and write his report of his findings on his remarkable journey, gathering information and experiencing the hardships and difficult conditions in the remote outback. He wrote hour after hour all through the night preparing that finely detailed report.

The Home Mission board, after receiving the report, presented it to the General Assembly of the Presbyterian Church of Australia and created intense interest and sympathy. Flynn's dreams were to come true when his suggestions were put to a group of prominent businessmen. The members of the Assembly who had never experienced travel or life in the outback moved more slowly than Flynn wished, looking into every detail. However his project was now in very capable hands and would move forward on a very solid foundation. The members of the assembly believed as Flynn did that the lives of mothers and babies were precious, and efforts would be made to eliminate the fear of young families in remote regions. They promised to build hospitals and improve transport and communication in the vast outback. The Assembly was confident the public would help by finding the money to build those hospitals. The board fired the first shots when Headquarters issued an appeal for five thousand volunteers in the cities all over Australia. They would carry the proud name of the Bush Brigade.

Their movement thereafter was quickly into action.

John Flynn was appointed Superintendent of Field Work. He immediately departed for Oodnadatta from

Adelaide in the little mixed train that crawled along on the 960 kilometre journey. It was a fortnightly train service, taking three days and nights for the journey. The passengers were a mixed lot: station managers, stockmen, railway workers, well sinkers and kangaroo shooters. John, with his easy style of communication, was soon on first-name terms with all on board the train. The encouragement each man offered John Flynn for the success of his dreams made him feel like he was walking on air.

Oodnadatta was the end of the line. John now felt it was time to stop talking and get on with the job. He rolled up his sleeves and with other volunteers started work clearing the ground to build the first nursing home. After twelve years work with the Smith-of-Dunesk Mission, the Presbyterian Church of Australia now controlled the ambitious dreams of Reverend John Flynn.

The Camel-man had shared many tragedies with many familes in the Outback. Each day he would dream of the changes he would one day make to comfort those affected. He really believed he would make those changes. Many people, upon hearing of his dreams, suggested that they were only dreams; it could never happen. He brooded over the necessity to travel by buggy on rough tracks from Alice Springs to Oodnadatta railhead to bring medical help to a sick person in pain, then place the critically ill patient on the train for another 970 kilometres to a hospital in Adelaide. Often they arrived at the hospital too late.

At times John Flynn was absent from his base at Oodnadatta for weeks and sometimes months. Many of his journeys covered thousands of kilometres by slow-moving camels.

Life went on in his absence. Mavis Bryant, a very dedicated and skilful nursing sister, had spent more than twenty years at various remote nursing homes in far outback country. Towards the end of a busy day she sat in her office at the Oodnadatta nursing home completing details and conditions of several of her patients who were recovering well and were at their convalescent stage. She had finished cleaning the wards and dispensary and had sorted the washing for the week ahead. With a sigh she lay back into her chair, relaxing after a typically hot, hard day's work.

The doorbell broke the silence. Two young girls with their aboriginal parents complained of sore eyes. Sister could see at a glance that the children were suffering from sandy-blight, a very common complaint in the region. She bathed their eyes and administered eyedrops and sent them on their way. Before she could sit back into her chair another patient arrived. An old Afghan camel-driver had received a nasty bite from a camel on his shoulder; she spent the next half hour washing and cleaning the bite, and administering a tetanus injection.

At last, just before midnight, Sister Bryant retired to bed for a well-earned rest.

Early next morning as the huge red sun came over the red sandhills to the east, the phone rang. It was a railway doctor travelling south with a construction gang. He was speaking from 200 kilometres away down the rail track at William Creek. "Child sick; serious; can you come?"

Sister Bryant paused, her two patients, although convalescing, still needed care and meals. One of the fettlers wives on these occasions volunteered to help. She would care for the patients in Sister's absence.

"Coming," she shouted over the phone. She packed a basket and hurried across to the railway line. A linesman was waiting there with a government railway motor trolley. Once aboard, the rails clicketty clacked under the small wheels of the trolley, and with the motor chug, chug, chugging, echoing into the misty morning air. With no windbreak or backrest and a sharp cold wind blowing into her face and hair, she tried to enjoy the experience of speeding the never ending steel strip stretching out in front. Frequently the sound of the wheels on rails reverberated as the speeding trolley crossed numerous bridges. The Algebuchina Bridge of 750 metres indicated the severity of the flooding waters on the many watercourses along the way.

Sister Bryant watched the passing scene of the desert

countryside with only a few Mulga and Gidgee trees now and then to relieve the monotony of the lightly grassed gibber plains. Dead stock lay along the dry riverbeds where they had died in their search for water. Occasionally a herd of wild wandering goats and a few root-grubbing rabbits ran from the approaching trolley.

The small railway siding of Mount Dutton came into view and a welcome stop was made. Sister was pleased to be able to stretch her legs and enjoy a cup of tea and a brownie offered by the wives of the local fettlers.

All along the railway track the gangs knew the mercy mission was coming, as they followed the progress of the motor trolley by listening on the railway phone. After a short stop they were once again speeding on their way to the next planned stop at Ann Creek, a further 75 kilometres on. There a very short stop was made as they were anxious to make William Creek before dark. After a tiring journey on the rough-riding trolley for eight hours, covering 200 kilometres, they finally arrived at their destination.

Sister immediately examined the sick child and ascertained a case of influenza, however not life threatening. She administed some soothing tablets to ease the coughing and instructed the mother to keep the child in bed for a few days.

Mrs Whitten offered a room for the night and Sister

gladly accepted the offer. After a hot meal she was thinking of going to bed when a horseman came cantering into the camp. He stopped in front of the house with an urgent message: a man was lying seriously injured with broken ribs and probably internal injuries some 75 kilometres out at a wild horse and brumby breaking camp. Was there a possibility of medical help?

Half an hour later, Sister climbed onto a wagonette. With no time to spare, Harry the driver let the horses plunge forward as he clung to the reins with his foot ready near the brake pedal. He stared into the dark gloom ahead as a misty rain fell – it had arrived at a most unwelcome time. Visibility was so bad they could hardly see the horses, let alone the bush track ahead. Before departing William Creek one of the fettlers had given Sister an oilskin railway coat for which she was now very grateful as the unseasonable heavy rain continued to fall.

Suddenly the two horses cantered into a large pool of water covering the track, and the water splashed up, blinding both the driver and Sister Bryant. The horses missed the turn in the track and charged into the bush, causing the wagonette to bounce over spinifex clumps and nearly capsize. The driver strained on the reins with all his strength and jammed his foot hard on the brake pedal, bringing the terrified horses to a halt.

Fighting to control herself, Sister pretended to be unconcerned at the unexpected event. The driver, who seemed unaffected, asked Sister to take the oil lamp and jump down and walk ahead to see if she could find the track. By criss-crossing ahead about 100 metres she located faint tracks that she hoped were the right ones. She signalled the driver by moving the light from side to side.

Once back on the track the horses seemed to realise the dangerous conditions and trotted slowly on. The increasing rain began to create problems with visibility and with the softening of the ground the narrow wheels of the wagonette were sinking into the track.

As they travelled over a gravel patch on a hillside their speed increased once again as the horses broke into a fast canter. Without warning they ran into another large pool of water on the track, missed a turn and careered into a creek which had mud deposited in the creek bed two metres deep. The horses ploughed through the mud, slipping and sliding as they staggered up the opposite bank. When the front axle struck the mud and the front wheels sank deep the wagonette stopped with a severe jolt. They were bogged up to the floorboards.

Both the Harry the driver and Sister Bryant climbed down from the vehicle and sank into the mud. The horses still strained on the traces but could not move the buggy. Harry had no alternative but to unhook the horses and lead them away from the boggy ground and tie them to a tree.

The two wet, muddy and unhappy travellers climbed

back onto the wagonette and sat within the only shelter they had, their oilskin coats, to await the arrival of the soggy dawn.

Daylight presented a hopeless scene. Harry and Sister looked at each other. He looked to the right and then to the left, and with a comforting grin said, "Well, Sister, I don't see anyone else around here to get us out of this bog so we had better get busy and get ourselves out."

One of the implements always carried on the back of wagons was an axe to be used on such occasions. The driver from his many years of experience with outback travel had been forced to extricate wagons and drays from such bogs many times. His first action was to cut a tree branch approximately 20 centimetres thick and 4 metres long. After cutting another two 2-metre saplings with forks, he placed these along the front of the wagonette in line with the wheels. The back wheels were still on hard ground.

"Now Sister," he said, "when I place this long pole over the axle hub of the back wheel and under the axle hub of the front wheel, I will bear down on this long pole and it will lift the wheel up. I will then need you to push this forked pole along to the back wheel. Then I will let the wheel down onto the pole that you have pushed along to the back wheel. I will repeat the same operation on the other side of the wagonette. We will then corduroy along the top of the two poles with short cut saplings. Hopefully, Sister, the horses should easily pull the wagonette free of that confounded bog."

As the driver suggested, the wagon was pulled clear with little effort. However, now both Harry and Sister were covered with red mud from head to foot. They sat down on a log, looked at each other and, in relief, they both laughed.

The laughing stopped abruptly as from behind and up the bush track came the sound of a galloping horse. The rider reined in his horse near the two sitting on the log in all their muddy glory. He laughed as he said, "Well you two make an interesting couple."

The driver replied, "Tom, you old bugger, I'll bet you were hiding around the bend when we were working like hell to get this wagon out."

"Oh Harry, you know I'm not like that. Anyway my mate's just back along the track, he's bringing the injured man along on a dray."

Shortly after, the dray arrived with the man lying on a roughly made stretcher. Obviously he was uncomfortable, but appeared quite cheerful and relieved when he saw Sister approaching to take charge of the situation.

"Now Harry, I want you to take that leather cushion from the wagonette seat and lay it on the floor. We will make the injured man a little more comfortable by not using that rough stretcher."

In the meantime, Tom had taken from the dray a

waterbag and a billycan to boil up a cup of tea. Sister was also grateful for Tom's offer of a little water and a basin to wash some of the mud from her face and hands. With Sister issuing instructions, the two men lifted the injured man tenderly onto the leather seat on the floor of the wagonette. Slowly the journey back to the railway commenced. From William Creek siding, the railway motor trolley completed another arduous mercy mission and returned to Oodnadatta Nursing Home. Sister Mavis Bryant could hardly remember when she last slept; maybe, she thought, fifty hours ago.

This is a typical example of the life of the gallant Bush Nursing Sisters in the remote Australian Outback.

When John Flynn returned and heard this story, he sighed about these distances. How could they be eliminated? Money, money, money; there was always a shortage of money. Hospitals should be available every few hundred kilometres throughout the outback. We must strive to establish them.

John believed firmly that the people of the metropolitan area would surely be happy to assist if they were made aware of the problems. He set out to make plans to visit some of the cities to give lectures and relate some of these experiences which he saw almost daily. He had taught himself photography and intended to use his photos in his lectures.

Communication was another important requirement. John Flynn had been watching the development of the magic of Marconi and his wireless invention. By 1923 the government had set up a wireless transmitting station at Wave Hill cattle station in the East Kimberley. This transmitted Morse code messages over long distances. However the equipment required for this service was cumbersome and extremely expensive. What John had in mind was a transmitter and receiver wireless that was small and inexpensive so that every remote homestead could afford to communicate with neighbours and to receive medical advice from doctors in emergencies. Radio experts dismissed his imagined wireless transmitter/receiver, which he called a Baby Transmitter, as folly. However nothing would convince him that a Baby Transmitter could not be built.

Even so, he admitted that the government transmitter at Wave Hill would be a great help. The telegraph line stretching from Darwin to Adelaide had been responsible for saving many lives. Every few hundred kilometres a little transmitting station operated by one postal employee tick-tacked a doctor in Adelaide the symptoms of a patient. He then received the advice for the treatment of the patient.

The Camel-man looked out across the plain with concern in his eyes. "These are modern days," he thought, "and yet only one telegraph-wire, and mailmen driving camels, represent the only means of communication in central Australia."

Most urgent is the building of hospitals and nursing homes. Then staffing the hospitals and nursing homes with trained medical staff.

However, Flynn's dreams didn't end there. Still to come was a Baby Transmitter for each homestead and a wireless network throughout the outback. Hopefully some day a flying doctor service would eliminate fear in remote locations for every mother and father in the outback. Motor transport was now looking a possibility and Flynn kept an interested eye on the advancement of aeroplanes.

Near the end of the First World War, John received a letter from Flying Officer Clifford Peel when he was discharged from the Australia Air Force. He set out in detail how John's dream of a Flying Doctor for outback Australia could be realised. Flying Officer Peel suggested in detail the suitable types of planes that could be used. Also the costs and reliability, petrol consumption and distances of operation from bases. He was certainly encouraged when plans in 1920 were being outlined for an air service to be called the Queensland and Northern Territory Aerial Service: QANTAS.

By 1926 Australian Inland Mission nursing homes or hospitals had been built at Oodnadatta, Beltana, Maranboy, Birdsville, Innamincka, Alice Springs and

Port Hedland. From the start of operations with the board Flynn put pressure on the board members to think modern, up-to-date and big with all aspects of management. He suggested motor vehicles instead of camels and to build modern hospitals instead of renting old sheds. All the board members listened patiently and almost always agreed with John's suggestions.

When they thought they could afford it, they gave John a second-hand Dodge utility for his long-distance patrols, instead of his camels. After taking possession of the Dodge, John immediately set about pulling the car to pieces, totally dismantling the motor to familiarise himself with its working parts. He needed to understand the mechanics in case it broke down in the remote outback.

With his motor vehicle John did many more patrols in a much shorter time. This also allowed to go on lecture tours to interest more people in his project as well as raising more money.

At the completion of each lecture tour, the correspondence increased tenfold, requiring many days office work answering letters and in some cases office girls offering to help out on their days off or after their working hours. These offers of help were gratefully accepted. Eventually so many girls offered to help that a system evolved that was called Office Teams. The office teams began a roster, which meant John was totally exempt from any office work.

The Church then encouraged every state in Australia to adopt the Office Team system, which also encouraged the recruitment of many more helpers volunteering for other duties. One of John's dreams of an army of helpers had now come true. The volunteer helpers throughout Australia number in the thousands.

The OTs, as they became known, were so numerous that state councils were established to manage the OTs in each state. No longer was John required to be involved in the office work of this huge organisation. At last he was free to apply all his energies to the task of developing his dream of a Baby Transmitter.

John travelled to Adelaide and became deeply involved with the intricacies of wireless telegraphy. He now presented himself as a learner radio amateur who desired the expert help of an experienced wireless adviser. He needed someone to build a transmitter/receiver radio set, inexpensive, light and simple so that every bush mother could operate it.

The wireless men he contacted could not resist his enthusiasm and belief that man can do anything. Several wireless experts seriously set to work to try to make his dreams come true. During their experiments they attracted the curiosity of a young wireless wizard. This young man lived for the excitement of wireless experimentation and invention. Mr Kauper, an Adelaide businessman, introduced Alfred Traeger to John Flynn, who in no time had Traeger immersed in experiments to solve John's dream of a Baby Transmitter.

As his newfound friends struggled with problems associated with the building of the radio set, John was invited to join the leading figures associated with Qantas Airways Service celebrations after operating for one year. Qantas had flown 350,000 hours without the slightest mishap. The dream of a flying doctor service was coming within his reach.

After spending a week in Sydney attending a board meeting with the full board of Home Missions discussing future plans, he caught a train to Adelaide. He joined Alfred Traeger and both proceeded to Alice Springs with Traeger's first Baby Transmitter radio for trials. Alf Traeger explained to John that Mr Kauper had assisted him in building the Baby Transmitter by utilising a crystal control. The need for a heavy generator was one of the problems that they would have to overcome. The generator created a fluctuating current, that was produced by uneven turning and consequently the signals were unreadable.

On arrival at Alice Springs John chose the hospital as their radio base. He then recruited two trusted friends to assist with the trial. He set up their small transmitting and receiving set, in what John called the Radio Room at the hospital. He instructed his friends on the operation of the set and gave them the scheduled time of the trial.

Traeger and John drove the 130 kilometres to Hermannsburg Mission Station and installed their set.

At the appointed time for the trial to begin, John nervously adjusted his earphones. He tapped the keys. The group of Lutheran missionaries, Traeger and John listened breathlessly. Silence. There was nothing, not a sound. John tapped again. Silence prevailed. In desperate disappointment, they abandoned the trial.

Arriving back in Alice Springs, Traeger and John rechecked the set, however they could find no reason for the failure. In desperation they decided to give it one more trial. They drove to Arltunga, seventy miles north-east from Alice Springs, and set up their transmitting set in the police station. At the appointed time once again John adjusted his earphones and strained to listen for a dot-dash from their friends in Alice Springs. Once again disappointment, although John was convinced he heard a very slight buzzing sound. That gave him enough confidence to continue with the struggle, with more work to achieve his goal.

It was back to Adelaide to work very long hours every day for twelve months. After dismantling the transmitter, Traeger discovered one of his mistakes for the failure of both trials. He had chosen the wrong coil for the receiver. After several months, John was required to leave the experiments to Traeger and return to attend board meetings in Sydney, where plans were being made to look more closely at the progress and development of Qantas air servies for the possible introduction of John's Flying Doctor Service dream.

The nursing home at Birdsville was also nearing completion. It was with tremendous pride and joy that John Flynn officiated at the opening of this new vital facility. The comfort given to remote families was stretching over vast distances of the outback, from Port Hedland in Western Australia to the Kimberley, the Northern Territory and South Australia. Now Birdsville in southeastern Queensland had completed the chain.

Once again John turned his attention to the Baby Transmitter he considered urgently required to complete the feeling of security in these outback regions. John was impatient to return to Adelaide to join Traeger to advance the work on the transmitter.

However, first John had to attend a meeting arranged by the Board with Mr HV McKay, the man who assisted materially in promoting Western Australian Airways Ltd, the very first operating air service in the country. McKay's advice was to go forward slowly with his dream of a Flying Doctor Service until aerial mail service routes were established and radio communication was more reliable. McKay advised that the success of the Flying Doctor would depend on rapid communication. John Flynn agreed with that advice, making it doubly important to get back to Adelaide to work with Traeger on the

Baby Transmitter.

Many experiments were conducted with many failures. Finally both men felt it was time to travel back to Alice Springs to trial their new set. Final instructions and a schedule were given to the Missionaries at Hermannsberg.

Almost every person living at Hermannsberg, the Missionaries and nomad aborigines crowded into the room hoping to witness whiteman's magic. At the appointed time, John nervously adjusted the earphones and took a deep breath, clasped his hands together as if in prayer, and then tapped the keys to register Morse code.

–•• (D) – – – (O) –•– – (Y) – – – (O) ••– (U)
•–• (R) • (E) •– (A) –•• (D) – – (M) • (E)

Hermannsburg replied:

•–•• (L) – – – (O) ••– (U) –•• (D) •– (A) –• (N)
–•• (D) –•–• (C) •–•• (L) • (E) •– (A) •–• (R)

Flynn and Traeger shook hands and embraced.

"We've got it!" Flynn exclained. "The Inland Speaks!"

When the excitement of the moment passed, John Flynn clapped his hands and said, "Right Alfred, back to work, we've a long road in front of us yet."

Alf Traeger returned to Adelaide and John made his way back to Sydney. He explained to the board the success of the Baby Transmitter in trials at Alice Springs and urged them to make haste with plans for the introduction of the Flying Doctor Service.

Traeger knew his job was not yet finished. To complete his task he had to find a way to discard the large, heavy and expensive generator and find a more mobile, light generator. Months went by and he found that each attempt to construct a light machine failed. Every minute of the day he pondered this question. He sat at his drafting table doodling as he watched the postman stop at his letterbox. There, that's it. On the front wheel of the postman's bicycle was a small generator to provide the light for night riding. The genius of Alfred Traeger soon became known the world over as the inventor of the pedal radio transmitter/receiver.

Shortly thereafter every family in their remote homesteads across the vast outback of Australia sat with earphones on and a foot pumping the pedal, a keyboard to connect and gossip with their neighbours or the outside world. Another of John Flynn's dreams had come true.

The Board formed a special Aerial Medical Service Committee with a sub-committee that consisted of very talented businessmen and army personnel. The Wool Brokers Association became involved and assisted with donations. The sub-committee, centred in Melbourne, was comprised of a number of experts in their special fields. Their job was to work out the problems that could be expected in association with the initiation of an aerial medical service. They were required to report if the service would be practical.

The Reverend John Andrew Barber, Honorary Convenor for the Victorian Council had been elected to be Patrol Organiser. The sub-committee ordered an investigation tour of 16,000 kilometres to meet and gauge the likely support for such a radical scheme. Reverend John Barber and Doctor George Simpson set off from Adelaide by motor vehicle and travelled north, visiting enroute Marree, Coober Pedy, Alice Springs, Tennant Creek, Maranboy, Katherine to Darwin, and many cattle stations in between. They continued via the Barkly Tablelands to Camooweal and Cloncurry (one of Qantas Aerial Services main bases). At Cloncurry they called a meeting and over 700 people came to voice their approval. Negotiations began immediately with Qantas in relation to leasing aircraft, cost, availability and other requirements for landing fields. Many station owners told the meeting that they had already prepared landing fields in anticipation of the aerial medical service that they hoped would be provided. Reverend Barber and Doctor Simpson were delighted with the signs of future success.

Right at the critical moment a case happened which proved the practical value of a flying medical service. An urgent request came from Mt Isa mines, 320 kilometres to the west, for a plane to transport a seriously injured miner to hospital in Cloncurry. Qantas pilot Phil Evans and Doctor Simpson flew out immediately. On arrival in Mr Isa, Doctor Simpson stabilised the patient and flew back to Cloncurry. This operation had placed the seriously ill patient in hospital in under three hours after the request for help. This timely event had a tremendous impact on the Boards members of the Home Mission. When it was relayed to the General Assembly of the Prebyterian Church of Australia, a Flying Doctor and Medical Service for Outback Australia was a done deal.

In May 1928 Doctor K St Vincent Welsh and pilot Arthur Affleck took off from Cloncurry airfield on the first official mercy flight that inaugurated the Aerial Medical Service.

In 1951 at the ripe old age of 94, Jim McGinty was sitting in his deckchair on the veranda of the Elizabeth Symon Nursing Home at Innamincka. His mind wandered back through the many reckless years of his youth. He had once worked at the Peake Cattle Station near Oodnadatta. He had ridden, broken in and educated wild brumbies and experienced many bad falls that resulted in broken bones. He remembered his first frightening experience of hard riding in the black of night to head off a rush of half-wild bullocks when his horse crashed to the ground right in the path of that crazy mob. Only a large rock that he was able to shelter behind saved him from being made into mincemeat.

Fresh in his mind after thirty years was the occasion when he was lying unconscious with malaria at Big Red, the sandhill east of Clifton Hills Station on the Birdsville Track when the timely arrival of his friend John Flynn saved his life.

The big red sun had disappeared over the desert sandhills and the soft twilight presented a relaxing picture of the beautiful red river gum trees lining Cooper Creek. Looking out across the vast red soil plains he could see a great cloud of red dust twisting and twirling as willy willies do. He watched, intrigued; he had never seen a bigger willy willy.

Suddenly he sat upright in his chair as he gazed intently at the bottom of the huge cloud of dust. He could clearly see the Camel-man on his camel with his prominent stooped back and his straight-stemmed pipe in his mouth. In a flash the red dust of the willy willy lifted high up into the sky. The Camel-man was gone.

Shortly after, Sister Clare Stewart appeared with an evening cup of tea. In a saddened voice she told Jim McGinty that she had just heard on the pedal radio that Reverend John Flynn had died.

VAUGHAN

# *Sidney Kidman, the Cattle King*

Near the town of Mannahill, out on the saltbush and bluebush plains of South Australia, several kilometres on the road between Adelaide and Broken Hill, lived a struggling family trying to establish a selection. The father, mother and three children had just begun to make headway on their property when a destructive drought struck, and at the same time cattle sheep and wool prices slumped.

The year was 1901, the year of Federation. On this particular day in mid-summer, with the heat haze dancing on the distant hills, the temperature was near 38°C.

The woman working at the well gritted her teeth in grim determination as she wound the handle of the windlass at the head of the well. Slowly the 25 litre bucket rose to the surface from 30 metres down. Still holding the handle of the windlass with one hand, she pulled the heavy bucket of water to the edge of the well mound and poured the water into a long trough. To her, it seemed like a drop in the ocean. She had been working at the well winding the windless for four hours to water the last remaining cattle and sheep, hoping they would survive the drought. Each and every day she had to do this work until the drought broke. Before lowering the bucket down the well once more the woman took a cloth from her belt to wipe the sweat from her brow. Her hands felt sore and stiff from winding the windlass.

As she lowered the bucket once more she glanced over to the modest slab home, just a short distance away. She was always fearful of fire. She could see her two youngest children playing under the gum tree. She knew the eldest daughter, an 8-year-old, would be inside the house preparing the midday meal. As she wound the bucket up once more from the bottom of the well her kelpie cattle dog, looked down the track towards the main road, stood up and barked. Glancing down the track she could see a two-horse wagonette in a cloud of dust coming towards her. The buggy stopped near the well. It was nicely fitted out with two beautifully groomed and well-bred horses, complimented with well-polished harness and brass fittings. A tall, well-dressed man jumped down from the wagonette and as he approached tipped his wide black hat and said, "Good morning, Missus. I was wondering if I could water my horses at your stock trough."

"You are welcome to do so," the woman replied.

He climbed to the top of the well mound and took the handle of the windlass from the woman.

"Then I'll wind the windlass a while to earn my horses a drink. It is a hot day," he said.

"Yes," she replied.

"You're lucky having a well like this. So well built."

He remarked, "It must have been a good well sinker."

"My husband," she replied. "He knows his job very well. Good timber-work in this well."

The thoughtful man then asked, "How come a woman like you is doing such hard work on such a hot day?"

"Because if I don't, the few remaining stock will die and we will lose our selection," she answered.

"Is your husband ill?" he questioned.

"No," she replied. "In these hard times my husband has to go away to the back country of New South Wales with a shearing team, to earn enough money for us to survive. The children and I must carry on without him for six months of the year."

As the man continued to turn the handle of the windlass, and tip the water into the trough, he suggested that by the time he had filled the trough he would need a cup of tea.

"How about you go over to the house and put the kettle on to boil."

He then pointed to the back of his wagonette and said, "In the back of my wagonette there is a box of food, biscuits, cake, tinned sausages, butter and tea. All sorts of things. Let's give the kids a bit of a picnic."

He smiled. "I don't need the food: I'll be in Broken Hill tomorrow night."

When he had filled the trough he walked over to the house where the woman had made tea and had scones on the table under the gum tree. The kindly man gave the children some sweets and played with them, pushing their swing. After saying to the woman that he thought the drought was about to break and that cattle and sheep prices should soon pick up, he stood up to continue his journey. As he drove away from the home both mother and children waved goodbye watching the wagonette disappear down the track in a cloud of dust.

It was just a week later, as the woman was at the well winding up the buckets of water to pour into the trough, that her dog stood up and barked. Looking down the track she could see a large wagon approaching, drawn by four large carthorses. On the wagon were a number of boxes, pipes and steel girders. The wagon stopped near the well and immediately the men jumped down and started to untie ropes holding the equipment. As they started unloading, fear touched the woman's heart. She rushed down to the wagon and said, "What are you men unloading? I have not ordered any machinery."

The man raised his head and said, "We have brought the windmill and pipes lady."

"I've ordered no windmill," she said. "We haven't got any money to pay for a windmill."

"Well, maybe not, missus," the man replied. "You don't have to pay for this windmill, but it certainly has to be delivered to this property. That's our orders, and the men to erect the windmill will be here in a few days."

"There must be some mistake," the woman replied. "Please don't unload it."

"Look missus, this is not the first time we've had to deliver something to a property that hasn't been ordered. I tell you missus, our orders are from Sidney Kidman. He watered his horses here last week."

"Who?" asked the woman.

"Sidney Kidman. You know missus, the Cattle King," came the reply.

It was still dark in the loft of a modest house in Adelaide. A boy shivered in the cold morning air. He knelt on one knee as he rolled his swag, with a threadbare rug and towel, along the floor. He then stood for a few seconds in a shirt, trousers, worn out boots and an old battered hat.

His serious eyes showed a grim determination, belying his fourteen years of age. He made not a sound as he touched his pocket and felt his five shillings – all he had in the world. Quietly he walked to the window of the loft. He dared not make a sound as his brother slept nearby and he would raise the alarm if he woke.

The night before, the boy had placed a ladder against the wall of the window which he now climbed down, and then walked over to the tree where he had tied his horse. He led the horse outside the gate and onto the grass near the road. After strapping his swag to the back of the saddle he swung up into it and sat there for a few moments thinking of his mother, whom he would never see again. With a lump in his throat he shook the reins and rode away into the dawn.

Young Kidman had worked at the Gepps Cross sale-yards since the age of ten for ten shillings a week. Of this amount he would give his mother four-and sixpence to help with the family bills. He retained sixpence a week to clothe himself and saved whatever he could. Over three years he had managed to save enough to buy an old one-eyed horse he called Cyclops. He paid 30 shillings for a bridle and saddle, and was left with only five shillings in his pocket. During the years that he worked at the sale yards the quietly-spoken lad had been a good listener. At every chance he would listen to the drovers, stockmen, cattle buyers and wagon-masters.

Always keen to learn, he met the big men of the bush and heard their stories about the big mobs of cattle in the outback and droving feats over long distances. He loved to listen to their stories of the great explorers Sturt, McDouall-Stuart, Burke and Wills, and Giles, all the men who found new grazing land that stretched to the far horizon and beyond. As he rode in the dawn light, the sun was coming up over the Mount Lofty ranges. Passing the outlying houses of Adelaide on his way to Gawler, he thought of the stories he had heard of the vast lands in the outback, and thought to himself: *somewhere out there, there must be a place for me.*

At lunchtime he rode into the small village of Gawler and bought a bun for a penny. After giving old Cyclops a drink, the boy proudly rode on into the rolling hill country. He had now covered 40 kilometres. Not bad he thought. The time had passed very quickly. He especially took note of the many horse teams harvesting the grain crops in the paddocks and the many wagons, carts and buggies carting the produce to the growing city of Adelaide.

He rode on into the afternoon and just before sunset he arrived at Kapunda, which meant he had covered 80 kilometres for the day. Not bad for old Cyclops, he thought. He booked into a boarding house for a bed, after making sure they had a stable for Cyclops and some chaff. The cost for the accommodation and two meals was 4 shillings, which he gladly paid after breakfast, leaving him with the princely sum of one shilling in his pocket. During the day, while travelling over rocky ground, old Cyclops showed signs of becoming lame. The boy dismounted and walked, leading his horse. As evening approached he started looking for a suitable camping site for the night. On reaching the top of a hill he saw a campfire in the bush, just off the road. As he approached and was about to pass the campfire a roughly clad man, just lifting a billy off the fire, glanced up. "Good evening boy," he said.

"Has your horse cracked up? Have you come far?" The boy answered both questions: "I've only come from Kapunda. I think he will be OK by tomorrow morning."

"Well, you had better come over to my campfire and have some of this wallaby stew I'm cooking. You can turn your horse out on to the good grass on the other side of the creek."

The boy gratefully accepted the invitation. He was not only tired but also cold and hungry. After the meal they both sat sipping a cup of tea. They chatted for several hours before unrolling their swags and turning in for the night.

The friendly man gave him some very good advice. He learnt that his newfound friend was a traveller from far off Western Australia who had been visiting the goldfields of Bendigo and Hill End to study the prospects for business. The man explained to the boy how the population exploded when new goldfields were found.

"It's always good to start a business when a new town is being developed." The man said. "Then grow your business as the town grows. Miners are always hungry for meat and all kind of supplies."

Kidman's mind was turning over as he tried to sleep, thinking of all the things he had learnt that evening. After breakfast the next morning he saddled his horse which had thankfully thrown off its lameness overnight. He thanked the travelling man for his hospitality as he held his hand out with one shilling to pay for the meals and the comfortable night by the campfire. The man said, "You're welcome laddie. You will need the money."

After riding for some time he came to the copper mining town of Burra. As he rode through the main street he tried to gauge the progress of the village. Maybe he could sell beef and horses here when he had his own cattle station.

Around midday he came across two men and a four-horse wagon stopped by the roadside. They were boiling a billy to make a cup of tea and have some lunch. Young Kidman recognised the men, whom he often met at the sale-yards where he had worked. The men waved and called out. "You're just in time for a cup of tea laddie. Better join us at the campfire."

Charlie Hayes and Harry Russell were drovers from

Mundi Mundi station. Kidman dismounted and walked over to join the men at the campfire. He was offered a piece of damper and a pannikin of tea.

"Where's a young'un like you heading out this way?"

"I'm going to Broken Hill to meet my brother George," the boy replied.

Charlie Hayes replied, "I heard your brother was at German Charley's place, Poolamacka station. You can come along with us if you wish." The boy gratefully agreed to work his passage by tailing the spare horses and gathering firewood when required. Now he was positive he would be able to meet up with his brother.

"Where did you get that bag of bones of a horse?" asked Charlie Hayes with a grin. "You'll never make a horse dealer."

The boy was silently resentful. He loved his old horse. It was all he owned in the world. "I bought him in Adelaide," he replied.

"Anyhow take your swag over to the wagon and keep the fire burning while we go over to the store and pub over there. I think you had better let us take your old horse over to the store. We'll buy him a feed of oats. Have the billy boiling when we return."

The two men walked away leading old Cyclops to the store. They promptly sold the horse for ten shillings and drank the money. Sometime later young Sid saw the men staggering back from the hotel. He looked anxious, as the men were not leading Cyclops. When he learnt that they had sold his horse he was heart broken. Cold with fury, and with a tear in his eye he looked across to the old bush pub and thought, *If that is what beer does to men then I will never let liquor touch my lips.* Sid Kidman never drank liquor in his life.

Over the next few days the boy walked behind the wagon looking after the spare horses and doing other chores to earn his keep. He thought a lot about men. He told himself he would never again trust a drinker and never ever take a man's honesty for granted. Day after day he trudged along behind the wagon. Each night, footsore and weary, he unrolled his swag and under the brilliant starry sky he lay awake listening to the men talking about the country they were passing through. He learnt about the value of saltbush and bluebush as stock feed and of the well-watered country they were now travelling through.

He learnt that this was the type of country Mundi Mundi station enjoyed. Long before they arrived at their destination he knew the carrying capacity of Mundi Mundi Station and other useful information for managing a large sheep and cattle station one day. A long way off the Barrier Ranges and the station homestead could be seen. That night as they were unharnessing the horses from the wagon Charlie Hayes mentioned he had a parcel he had to deliver to German Charley at Poolamacka

Station. He suggested to Sidney that he could come along with him and that he would lend him a horse to ride. Thereby he would meet his brother at Poolamacka Station another 150 kilometres further on.

On his arrival his brother George welcomed him with a lecture and abuse for running away from his mother and home. German Charley provided a welcome evening meal, cooked by greasy Jack the station cook. German Charley was a blue-eyed rogue that had developed Poolamacka station ten years before from scratch. German Charley noted that the lad had walked from Adelaide and was keen to find work, so offered him a job cutting wood and cleaning the pots and pans in the kitchen. Kidman gladly accepted. His pay would be his keep and accommodation.

After several months his brother George told him that he was going away on a droving job. He had secured Sid a job as a shepherd over at Harry Raines' place.

"You will find it really tough working for Mr Raines. He is a very hard man. You'll wish you were back with your mother," George told his young brother.

Harry Raines was a squatter. He held no country of his own, he just moved on with his sheep and three hundred cattle when the feed ran out. Over the next hill was another well-grassed valley, which he called his long paddock.

Young Sid was delighted when told his pay would be

eight shillings a week and keep. He counted up all the money he could save in a few months. He was not so happy however when he found out his accommodation was a cave in the side of a creek, which he shared with a young aboriginal boy called Willie. Willie was the first aboriginal Sid had ever known. The two got on really well. Willie taught Sid how to live off the land, and how to hunt and track animals, which was to prove useful in later years.

At times Harry Raines would take Sid away on horseback, searching for more grassed valleys to move his stock to when all the feed was gone at their present location. On these excursions Sid learnt a lot about the country. One day, over the hill and into the valley rode an aboriginal stockman droving a flock of sheep, followed by a large wagon driven by another man. Several spare horses followed close in the rear.

The man was Abraham Wallace, who had legally taken up the land on which Raines' sheep were grazing. An almighty row developed. However, Wallace legally owned it and Raines had to move on. Unfortunately young Sid lost his job. Wallace eventually developed the property into one of the finest sheep stations in the land and Sturt Meadow station is still producing quality wool today. Raines moved on to take up land legally where Mootwingee is today. Kidman rolled up his swag and whistled as he walked over the ranges towards Mount

Gipp Station about 40 kilometres away. In his pocket was a tightly rolled 25 pounds, which was his pay from Mr Raines. Little did he know that the very rough broken range he was walking over was a mountain of silver yet to be discovered.

On arrival at Mount Gipp station he introduced himself to the manager Mr George McCullough and asked for a job, which he got. He was now a rouseabout on a real station with over forty stockmen. The fit, strong and willing worker soon became a favourite with George McCullough, who continually gave him good advice and information about running the station.

One of his first jobs was to be a boundary rider. He rode his horse accompanied by another German lad named Charles Rasp. The boundary fence was over 120 kilometres long, and as they rode they had to fix any breaks in the fence. Each night as the two lads settled down at the campfire, Rasp would show Kidman the samples of rocks he had picked up throughout the day. He was an amateur geologist. One night Kidman said to Rasp, "Look Charles, I'm not interested in the rocks you gather each day. I'm only interested in the grass that grows between those rocks and from that grass one day I'll make a fortune."

"Maybe so," replied Rasp. "One day I'll make a fortune from those rocks."

A few years later Charles Rasp discovered the mountain of silver at the broken hill, that is now known as Broken Hill city. Rasp certainly became very rich indeed.

At Mount Gipp station, under George McCullough's instructions, Kidman learnt to break-in and educate young horses. But of course he learnt the hard way with many falls from frisky young horses. He made his first horse deal when he bought a horse in very poor condition from a passing drover for 30 shillings. With careful handling and some good feed, the horse's condition improved and he decided to keep the young chestnut colt for himself. He bought another horse in poor condition and once again improved its condition. He was unable to make a deal with this horse so he swapped it for two other horses. He more than doubled the 30 shillings he had paid for the original horse he bought. Many travellers and drovers often camped down near the front gate beside the road and Kidman would join them at their campfire and listen intently as the men talked of the country they had come through.

They told tales of their journeys through what they called the Three Rivers country of Queensland. The drovers explained to the lad that where those rivers flowed to, there must be huge flood plains. He thought a lot about these likely flood plains and decided he would go there some day to see for himself its condition. On another night as he sat quietly in the shadows of a campfire listening to drovers talking about their journey from the Lachlan river, one man mentioned that some prospector had discovered copper at a place they called Cobar.

"A town is rapidly being established there."

Young Kidman listened intently to this information. He remembered the kind man who had made him so welcome at his campfire. The travelling man from the goldfields of Western Australia had advised him to start a business if he ever heard of a new town being developed. He made a snap decision to go to Cobar. He resigned from his job at Mount Gipp station where George McCullough was sorry to see him depart. However, he wished him well in his new adventure.

With his swag strapped to his saddle on his beautiful chestnut colt he rode away on the track to Cobar – 400 kilometres to the east. A few days later he came across a droving team and bought another horse for a packhorse. After crossing the Darling River, he arrived in the bustling town of Cobar.

After deciding where he believed the main street was being formed he cut some saplings to build a brush shed. On selecting a chopping block from the bush he thought, *Now I've got a butcher shop, I need some meat.*

The nearest cattle station was 45 kilometres away. The next day he bought two bullocks, drove back to Cobar, slaughtered them and presented the meat for sale. The miners immediately rushed in and his meat sold out in a few hours. Kidman set off once again to the cattle station to buy more cattle. He offered to buy ten bullocks if the station owner would give him a good price.

He told the station owner he would come back almost weekly. He was given a bargain price and bought ten bullocks. A few weeks later he employed a lad to work in his butcher shop. Kidman invested in a bullock wagon, and when the mine in Cobar began to operate he won the contract to cart the copper ore to Bourke, for loading onto riverboats for transport to Port Adelaide. On returning from Bourke to Cobar his wagon was loaded with all the supplies needed for sale to the miners in Cobar, and therefore he had loading for his wagon both ways. Twelve months after starting up in Cobar, a Sydney businessman offered him one thousand pounds for his business. That night he tossed and turned in bed trying to decide if he should sell. In the morning he said to himself, *I don't want to be a shopkeeper all my life. I want to be a cattle station owner and cattle and horse dealer.* He sold his business that day.

With his swag once more strapped to the back of his saddle, he mounted his chestnut colt Prince, with a packhorse well loaded with food, and accompanied by his kelpie cattle dog Nelson he set off to follow his dream to explore the Three Rivers country of Queensland and search for those mighty flood plains.

He rode beyond Bourke following the Warrego River

to Cunnamulla and Charleville. Stopping to talk to drovers or cattle station owners, he gathered information about the region. Charleville in those days was the headquarters of Cobb and Co. stagecoaches and also the location of their factory for building coaches and wagons.

One station owner told of the terrible drought gripping the country out at Thargomindah. Kidman decided to travel out that way to look over the land. On arrival he met a cattle-station owner who was in fear of losing all his cattle in the drought. Kidman knew that the country over the border of New South Wales was still in good condition, unaffected by the drought. Kidman knew of some well-grassed valleys on the Bullo River floodplains. He took a chance and bought 500 head of the drought-affected cattle. Following the Bullo River, he spent a month on the well-grassed floodplains before continuing his journey to Broken Hill. He sold the cattle for top price, doubling his money once again. Now there was no stopping him. The rest of his life was spent dealing and breeding sheep, cattle, and horses, and owning cattle stations.

At this time he had good reason to visit Kapunda where a few years before he had taken a mob of horses for German Charley from Poolamacka station. On that occasion Kidman had met a young Scottish lass, the schoolteacher at Kapunda. He was keen to re-establish that friendship so Kidman, his horse Prince and dog

Nelson, adopted Kapunda as their home. Later that year he married Belle, the young schoolmistress.

One night after their evening meal, Sidney and Belle poured over a map of Australia on the kitchen table. He pointed out to Belle the three rivers that flooded into thousands of hectares on the plains of the Channel country of Western Queensland.

The Diamantina, Georgina and Cooper Creek were the key to his plans to establish a string of cattle stations from the Gulf country of Queensland to the markets in New South Wales, Victoria and South Australia. Using that method he was not forced to drive cattle thousands of kilometres to markets. His method would produce cattle for sale in the very top condition, thus bringing top prices.

Over the next four years Kidman developed his business a hundredfold. In partnership with Jimmy Nicholson he established a stagecoach and transport company.

In partnership with Thomas Elder, he established Owen Springs station, near Alice Springs. Several years later Thomas Elder sold Kidman his share of the station. Thus he owned his first station. The Kidman Company still owns Owen Springs today, more than one hundred years on.

It was not uncommon for Kidman to ride his horse on journeys of over four thousand kilometres or more.

He would visit his stations to arrange transport to market for his fat cattle, or buy cattle to stock the cattle stations he had established in the channel country of Queensland. He would organise droving teams to deliver cattle to markets in Adelaide along the remote Birdsville track.

Imagine him setting out on his horse or in a buggy to travel from Kapunda to Broken Hill to Bourke to Longreach to Burketown to Cloncurry to Birdsville and down the Birdsville track to Marree and finally back home to Kapunda. Kidman must have completed that journey many times, a distance of over 4000 kilometres.

In the years leading up to the First World War, Kidman owned 117 cattle stations stretching from the Kimberley of Western Australia through the Northern Territory and through the channel country of Western Queensland to New South Wales, Victoria and South Australia. At the beginning of the First World War Kidman provided free horses he had bred on his properties to the Australian Army for the Light Horse Brigade. Sidney Kidman also provided most of the meat eaten by our armed forces.

It would almost take another book to name all the Kidman cattle stations. Some of the more famous stations he owned were: Victoria River Downs, Mt House, Yeeda, Glenroy, Wave Hill, Elsey, Banka Banka, Newcastle Waters, Brunette Downs, Alexandria, Avon

Downs, Loraine, Fossil Downs, Owen Springs, Innamincka, Durham Downs, Sandringham, Pandi Pandi, Clifton Hills, Cordillo Downs, Bullo, Mt Gipp, Beltana and Wooltana. I could add another 93 to the list. This number represents the largest landowner in the world.

Transferring cattle from station to station, always moving them towards the markets, and thus arriving with cattle in top condition meant he always got top price for his cattle. Kidman gave many thousands of dollars to charity and he never forgot a friend.

He called Australia a friend and donated the very first fighter squadron planes to the Australian air force. Another friend was the legendary Rev. John Flynn, known as Flynn of the Inland. When establishing his famous Outback Flying Doctor service, Kidman donated his aircraft.

He and Belle had two daughters and a son. Today stretching far and wide across Australia are still many cattle stations showing the Kidman brand of efficiency.

In his mid seventies Sidney Kidman could still be found along the tracks of the outback checking on his cattle stations and the number of fats available for sale. Finally Kidman turned over the management of the cattle empire to his son Walter.

He could often be found sitting on his old seat at the saleyards at Gepps Cross with an old mate, guessing the prices certain mobs of cattle would bring at the sale. In

1936, at the age of seventy-nine, now honoured by the King of England, Sir Sidney Kidman was sitting on his old rocking chair on the front verandah of his house in the Mount Lofty Ranges.

He was looking down on the city of Adelaide, the little town he rode away from so long ago. He had been reading the morning newspaper, no doubt looking at the weather charts to see what the rainfall was likely to be on some of his stations. He had just finished a cup of tea that his loving wife Belle had given him, when suddenly the paper slipped from his fingers, and his head rested on his chest. His time had come to pass. When the word of the passing of Sidney Kidman was received in the far outback, all the station owners, stockmen, and drovers sitting around their campfires, well remembered the words they had often heard him say, "When my time is up, I'll roll my swag and ride off to the great flood plains in the sky".

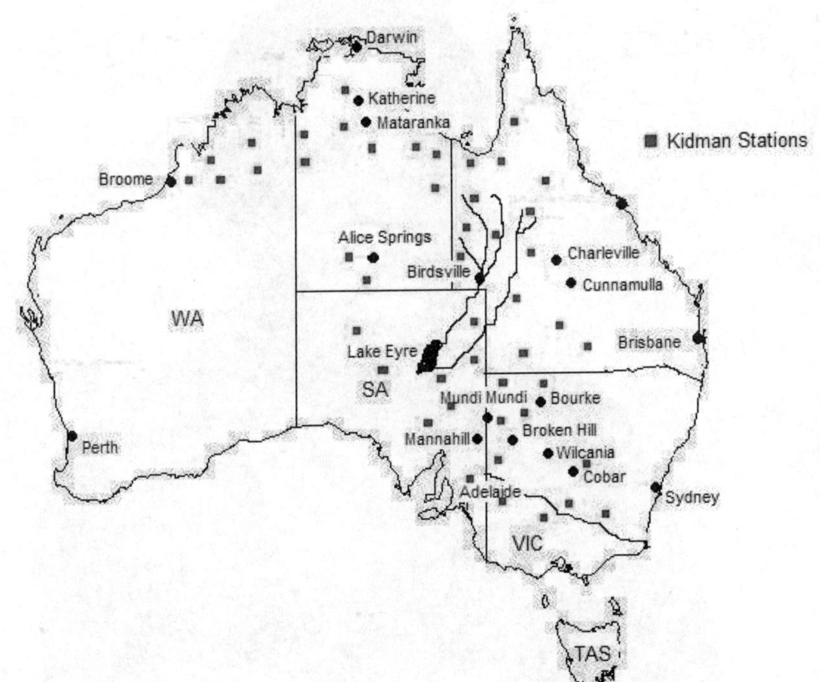

Darwin
Katherine
Mataranka
Kidman Stations
Broome
Alice Springs
Charleville
Birdsville
Cunnamulla
WA
Brisbane
Lake Eyre
SA
Mundi Mundi
Bourke
Broken Hill
Mannahill
Wilcania
Perth
Cobar
Adelaide
Sydney
VIC
TAS

Blanasi

# *Blanasi and his Didgeridoo*

A great Australian musician died on the 6 August 2001. Blanasi died in his tribal land in Arnhem Land, Northern Australia. You've never heard of him? What a shame! He was probably the greatest didgeridoo player, and a wonderful, talented entertainer. He enthralled his audiences around the world. Back in the early 1970s most Australians had never seen or heard the music of a didgeridoo or seen Aboriginal dancers. In 1971, I was commissioned by Woolworths of Sydney to travel to the wilds of Arnhem Land and organise a group of Aboriginal dancers to perform at the Waratah Festival in Sydney.

I knew Arnhem Land well, after many visits to that

country fishing and hunting with my young tribal friend, Blanasi. With his help I was able to gather the best 10 dancers in Arnhem Land. These 10 dancers, a song man, and a didgeridoo player formed the group on arrival in Sydney. Woolworths provided a semi-trailer. The Aboriginal dancers, with the song man and didgeridoo player, performed on the semi-trailer in full cultural dress, paints and feathers, mesmerizing tens of thousands of people along the route. Later that day they danced at a concert in Hyde Park. As a result of the huge success of that visit to Sydney the group and I were invited over the following years to perform at many major events.

Rolf Harris asked me if I would arrange for Blanasi and our song man to perform with him at the very first concert at the Sydney Opera House. This was another huge success. In the following year Rolf took Blanasi with him to perform at the Australia Day concert at the World Expo 74 in Spokane, Washington USA. After that concert Rolf told me Blanasi stole the show from the stars Helen Reddy and Judy Stone. Other notable engagements included, the Medical Convention of the South Pacific in Sydney, and the Rotary convention in Melbourne, both featuring Bobby Limb as Master of Ceremonies.

At times, when Blanasi came to Sydney for an engagement, I would meet him at the airport and he would always stay with my wife and I in our two-bedroom unit. He always called our second bedroom his camp. Being brought up in Arnhem Land in the 1950s–60s he never had the opportunity of school and hadn't learnt to read and write.

On one occasion when he came to Sydney I was not informed. A producer for a show at the Opera House required didgeridoo music to be taped for the show. The producers were advised to engage Blanasi. A native patrol officer found him in Arnhem Land and put him on a plane to Sydney. A representative of the show met him and took him to the Opera House so they could tape his music at the final rehearsal. After the rehearsal was finished at around midnight, the production manager said to Blanasi, "We have a taxi outside to take you to a hotel where we have booked a room for you. Our representative will call in the morning to take you to the airport for your return flight."

"Hotel!" Blanasi said, "I not go to no hotel. I go to stay with my blood brudder."

"Oh," said the manager, "have you a blood brother here in Sydney?"

"Yep," said Blanasi.

"OK," the manager said. "You just tell the taxi driver where to go. Thanks for coming." He handed Blanasi $100 in payment for his work. Blanasi went to the taxi.

"Where to mate?" the taxi driver asked.

"Wandwick."

"OK Randwick," the taxi driver confirmed. On arrival at Randwick the driver asked, "What street mate?"

"To my blood brudder Bert Bolton camp. I not know any street. You follow all these tracks and I find his camp." Blanasi had been to our place many times over the years. He soon recognised the Prince of Wales hospital in High Street. "Stop! Stop!" He paid the driver and walked across the road into the foyer and up the stairs to the third floor. He knocked on the door and a bloke came to the door with a towel around himself. Obviously he had been in the shower.

"Where is Bert?" asked Blanasi.

"Who?" the man said, "I don't know any Bert around here," and he slammed the door. He must have been shocked to find an Aboriginal man at his door at 1.30am. Blanasi went back down into the street and after concentrating he recognised our balcony. 'Now I'm right,' he thought as he went to the foyer entrance. The door was locked. He didn't know about the security system. Whenever I brought him home, I drove the car into the garage under the units, walked ahead of him, and with my key opened the door into the foyer and he would follow me up the stairs.

Now there he was at 1.30am locked out. So he sat down on the foyer steps thinking what to do next. He looked up at our window on the third floor where he knew we would be sleeping. My wife shook me.

"Bert wake up. Listen." I listened. I could hear softly, so softly, the playing of that beautiful haunting sound. *Did-gi-ma Did-gi-ma Did-gi-mee Did-gi-mee Did-gi-ma Did-gi-mee.*

I sprang out of bed looked down from our window and could see all our neighbours looking down at a little bloke playing his didgeridoo.

"Is that you Blanasi?"

"Yep Bert. Let me in."

Did I let him in? Yes of course, he was my lifelong friend, him my blood brudder. Blanasi slept in his camp that night, in our second bedroom.

Blanasi was an icon with a didgeridoo. During the 1960s and '70s he was the greatest didgeridoo player in the world. When in the company of other Aboriginal didgeridoo players, they would be too shy to play in his presence. Most would be over-awed in his company.

He travelled the world on a number of occasions to produce his wonderful music at concerts and TV shows. He performed in the company of many great stars in the entertainment world.

Like all great artists Blanasi, captured the hearts of his audience immediately he walked on stage. He possessed stage mastery with his inimitable style and wonderful smile. His music was unique and magic. His audiences loved to hear him tell his story as a boy in Arnhem Land learning to play a didgeridoo.

"Father and my grandfather play wonderful didgeridoo music. Even before my grandfather. A long way back our family play didgeridoo. We bin music makers of the tribe. When I was little kid, maybe 5, my father give me a little didgeridoo and he says, "Blanasi you must learn to play didgeridoo now." I start to practise and make a lot of noise. All the people say, "Shut up you make too much noise. You will never be able to play like your grandfather or your father." I feel sad. I go away in bush to little billabong and I blow and I blow and the sound came. I blow some more and the sound him better. Soon I can play good and I listen to the bird's sing and the dingo (wild dog) call. I play bird song and dingo call with my didgeridoo. I go back to tribe and say to my father. "Now I can play didgeridoo good like you. More than that I can play bird song, and dingo call." I play didgeridoo better than my father. He only plays in Arnhem Land. I play in London, Paris, New York, all over the world."

Yes, Blanasi did play his didgeridoo music all over the world. He and I went to New Zealand to visit all the main cities and large country towns on a one night stop promotional tour for the Northern Territory Tourist Association.

On arrival at the Christchurch airport he and I were ushered into the interview room. The television interviewer, indicated to Blanasi to sit in the chair behind one of the microphones. Blanasi looked at me with a smile and pointed to the chair. I said, "No, he wants to interview you, not me." He sat down. The room was full of other newspaper and radio reporters. The interview began, the TV evening news cameras rolled.

"Mr Blanasi, welcome to the land of the long white cloud," Blanasi looked a little puzzled and looked up to me and grinned. "Now Mr Blanasi, I understand early this morning you got in a small plane and flew from the wilds of Arnhemland to the town of Darwin. There you got on a bigger plane to go to Alice Springs and then to Sydney. In Sydney you got on a great big Jumbo plane and you flew away across that big sea to here, to Christchurch New Zealand.

"Now that must be some adventure for you. Tell me Mr Blanasi, have you ever been to big towns like Darwin or Alice Springs or Sydney before?" Blanasi looked up at me with a smirk and a twinkle in his eye. He looked back at the interviewer, then looked directly at the TV camera and said, "Yep, Ah been to Darwin, and Ah been to Alice Springs, and Ah been to Sydney, AND Ah been to Karachi, Ah been to Paris, Ah been to London, and Ah been to New York. Ah been all over the world." The interviewer looked embarrassed and red faced. He hadn't done his homework on the man he was sent to interview.

"Well, well, Mr Blanasi you have certainly been to more places than I have." The interview ended with roaring laughter made by the other reporters.

Blanasi was the complete professional and enjoyed the joke and he played it to a treat.

We did a promotion at Dunedin in the South Island of New Zealand. The organisers of the promotions had a car and driver to take us to the next venue in Invercargill.

We departed Dunedin very early on a frosty morning and we encountered ice on many corners of the road, occasionally we could feel the car slip and slide and I was concerned the driver was travelling too fast for the conditions. Blanasi sat back enjoying the slides quite unconcerned.

Invercargill is approximately 175 kilometres from Dunedin, however we arrived safely. The next day we were flying from Invercargill to Wellington. During the flight I read in the daily newspaper a story about a transport driver driving a two-deck sheep truck, loaded with two hundred sheep, along the icy road we had travelled on the day before. The truck swerved and slid on an icy bend and crashed through a bridge into deep water and the driver was killed. I remarked to my friend, "Heck if we had slid on that ice when that bloke was driving so fast yesterday, we may have been killed".

"No matter, Bert," he casually replied. "We go back to our tribal land just the same."

In the Aboriginal world they are strong believers in reincarnation. Their spirit goes on forever.

In 1973 both Blanasi and I were assisting Rolf Harris during his rehearsals for the first concert at the Sydney Opera House. During a break in rehearsals I mentioned to Rolf that later in the year my Aboriginal friend and I were going on a journey through the remote country of Arnhemland to meet his family and members of his tribe.

"Hey, can I come?" Rolf asked enthusiastically. I hastily warned him that we would be travelling native style walking and living off the land. "That'll be pretty rugged with no mod cons." After the excitement of the concert had been completed, we were all in the Green room (the artists private lounge) having a few celebratory drinks, when Rolf breached the safari again. "Now let's talk about that trip you two are planning. What's it all about, and when is it happening?" he asked.

"We plan to leave Darwin in May after the wet season up there." I replied. "It is impossible to travel in that country during the wet season which is November to May."

Rolf explained that he was returning to London the next day, He would check his future engagements with his manager back in London. "I would love to do that before I get too old," he said.

After a number of letters between Rolf in London, and me in Sydney we decided to meet in Darwin 20th May. 1973. The men taking part in this adventure were three white men: Rolf, my mate of many years; Harry Ellis; and myself. The three tribal men were: Blanasi, Willy Oenpelli and Left Hand Paddy. At that time Arnhemland had not been modernised as it is today. There were no made roads and the native people still lived as they had for thousands of years. Their houses were mainly bark huts built on stilts to escape the wet or brush huts on the ground.

Since the initial plan was to walk the whole journey, we changed that because Rolf was limited to a three week absence from his London engagements.

I hired a Nissan four-wheel drive station wagon.

Harry and I picked Rolf up when he cleared customs and set off 300 kilometres south to the Aboriginal settlement of Bamyili (now Barunga), a modern Aboriginal village with streets and real houses, a general store and sport shed for basketball and a grassed football ground. There, we were to meet my three Aboriginal friends.

Having gone without sleep on his long flight from London, Rolf climbed into the back seat of the vehicle and slept for next couple of hours as we drove south. On arrival at Katherine, Rolf woke up and said, "Is this our last opportunity to stock up all the necessary food for our journey?"

I said, "Hey Rolf, we are supposed to be living off the land on this journey Aboriginal style."

"OK," he replied, "I just thought we might need a

bit of insurance in case there are no kangaroos or we can't catch fish."

Harry and I both relented and followed Rolf into the general store. An old style store where the storekeeper is behind the counter and collects the order from the shelves and deposits them on the counter. I watched with interest at Rolf's selections, weeties, corn flakes, powdered and condensed milk, tins of bully beef, baked beans and spaghetti. As we started to carry the boxes of food out to the vehicle, Rolf called out, "Would you blokes like an ice cream?"

Harry looked at me strangely and said, "I had one of them many years ago. Oh I guess so, I'll be with you Rolf. I'll have one thanks."

I answered, "Yes, mate I'll have an ice cream. Thanks."

Shortly after we got the shock of our lives at the totally unexpected result of our decision. Actually we were being introduced to the normal unexpected, travelling with this guy.

Rolf came out of the store with three litres of ice cream, one each. "I just love ice cream," he announced as he passed each of us a litre container.

He then sat down in the gutter and we joined him to gorge on ice cream.

The scene for the public as they passed by, created much interest, not only to see three grown men sitting in the gutter eating a container of ice cream, but surprised to see that one of those blokes was the famous Rolf Harris. Soon a crowd gathered to talk and seek autographs. No not from Harry and me!

We continued our journey another 100 kilometres to Bamyili and were loudly welcomed by what seemed like dozens of the kids. Most of the kids knew me and some of the older kids knew Rolf because he had been there a few years before when making a documentary for the BBC.

Bamyili was the appointed place to meet our three Aboriginal friends. We looked around but could not spot them. We saw people going into and coming out of the general store so we went in there to ask where the fellows might be found. Inside Rolf said, "You fellers want another ice cream?"

We yelled back, "No!"

The storeman told us to look in the local club shed. Beer was available to buy from 2pm till 4pm. However it had to be drunk in the clubhouse. We strolled over and there they were, each had a can of VB in their hand. Much hugging and handshaking took place. Then Blanasi in a loud voice called, "Hey fellers, come and meet my friend Rolf Harris, do you remember him? He's the bloke with the three legs." It was a general invitation to anyone within earshot. Rolf on his last visit had performed his little skit of Jake the Peg with his extra leg.

Harry and I had a beer and Rolf a soft drink whilst we talked over our plans to depart Bamyili tomorrow morning. After that gathering we departed the clubhouse to select a spot in the bush just out of town, to put up our tents for the night. We each had an airbed and sleeping bag with mosquito nets, as the mossies are vicious in Arnhemland. We three were invited to dine at the storekeeper's house that night. We met our three other friends early next morning to begin our big adventure.

With all the extra food Rolf had bought and our own supplies and cooking utensils, along with a four-gallon drum of petrol we were really pushing for room. With one man driving and two others sitting in the front, that left only room for two men on the back seat, as we had loaded a lot of the food boxes also on the back seat. This vehicle had a canvas roof so we could not employ a roof rack. So we both looked at Engineer Harry.

"OK," Harry responded. "I'll build a platform on the back step under the back door." This he did, the platform was about 50 centimetres wide and stretched across the back about two metres. This allowed us to strap the drum of petrol on the end of the platform, and still left room for two blokes to stand and hang on to the frame of the canvas roof. This arrangement worked well as we all took it in turns on the platform, which we enjoyed.

Departing Bamyili about 8.30am, we had a crowd of about fifty men women and children shaking our hands and cheering as I revved the motor to indicate the start of our journey.

Travelling on a reasonable track we crossed over the Waterhouse River near the small neighbouring Aboriginal settlement of Beswick. Again we were greeted with an excited crowd as they had been warned to expect us. Our three friends had many relatives there, and they greeted each other as if they hadn't seen one another for years. I believe it had been about one week.

We had to insist that we had to continue our journey, as our three men seemed to be making themselves at home with their relatives. I thought we would never get away. By now it was nearly 4pm, and we made our way along a very sandy track and forged across, once again the top end of the Waterhouse River into Beswick Lagoon, into which the Beswick falls flowed in a wonderful display of rainbow colours as the last of the sun's rays reflected on the cascading water.

The lagoon took our attention as we sat on the sandy beach admiring the tranquil scene. The lagoon seemed to be alive with fish jumping high out of the water and crashing back to disappear under water. Blanasi ventured to explain, "It's feeding time for the large Barramundi and the little mullet are jumping because they don't want to get eaten. But the Barramundi always win."

Just when we thought the scene couldn't get better, there came the large full moon rising directly above the

Rolf Harris and Blanasi in Spokane, Washington
for an Australia Day concert.

Blanasi and Bert fishing in Arnhemland

Coopers Creek – scene similar to where Burke died

Bert and the searchers

McArthur river

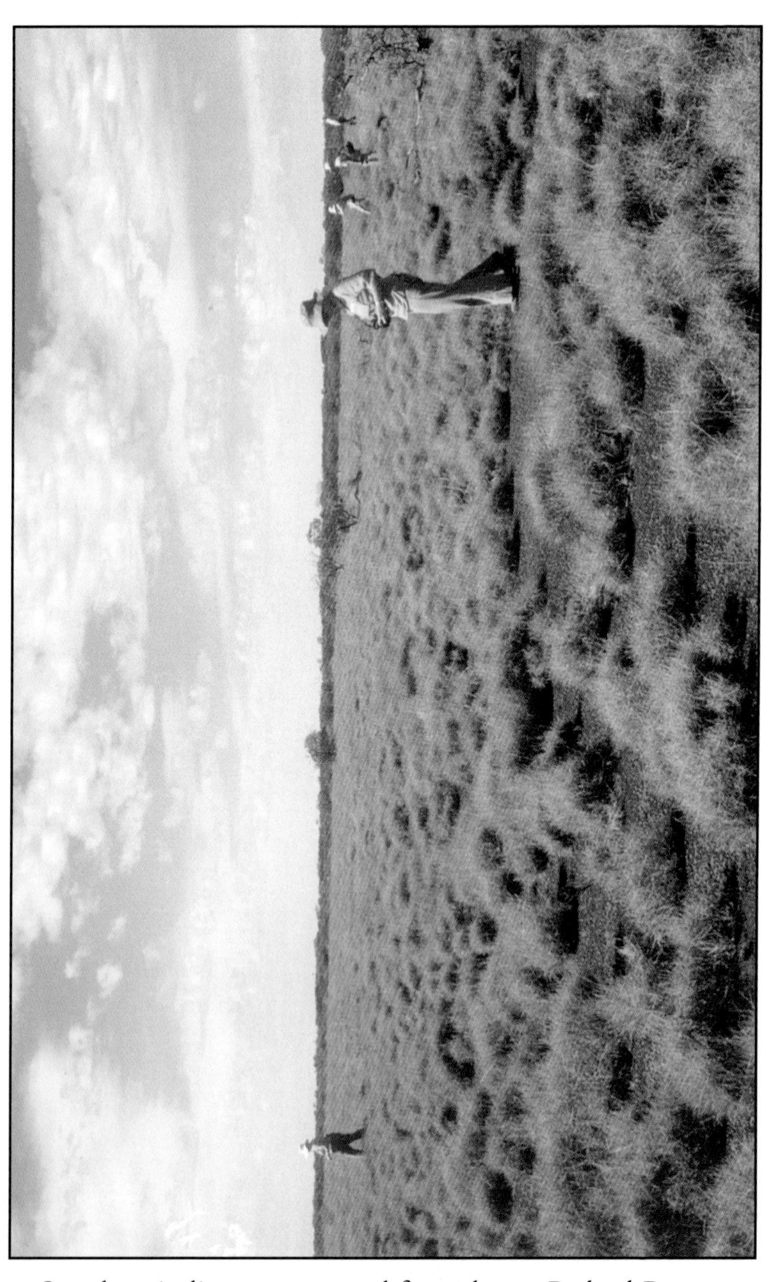

Searchers in line across gravel fround near Bedrod Ranges

Gibson desert

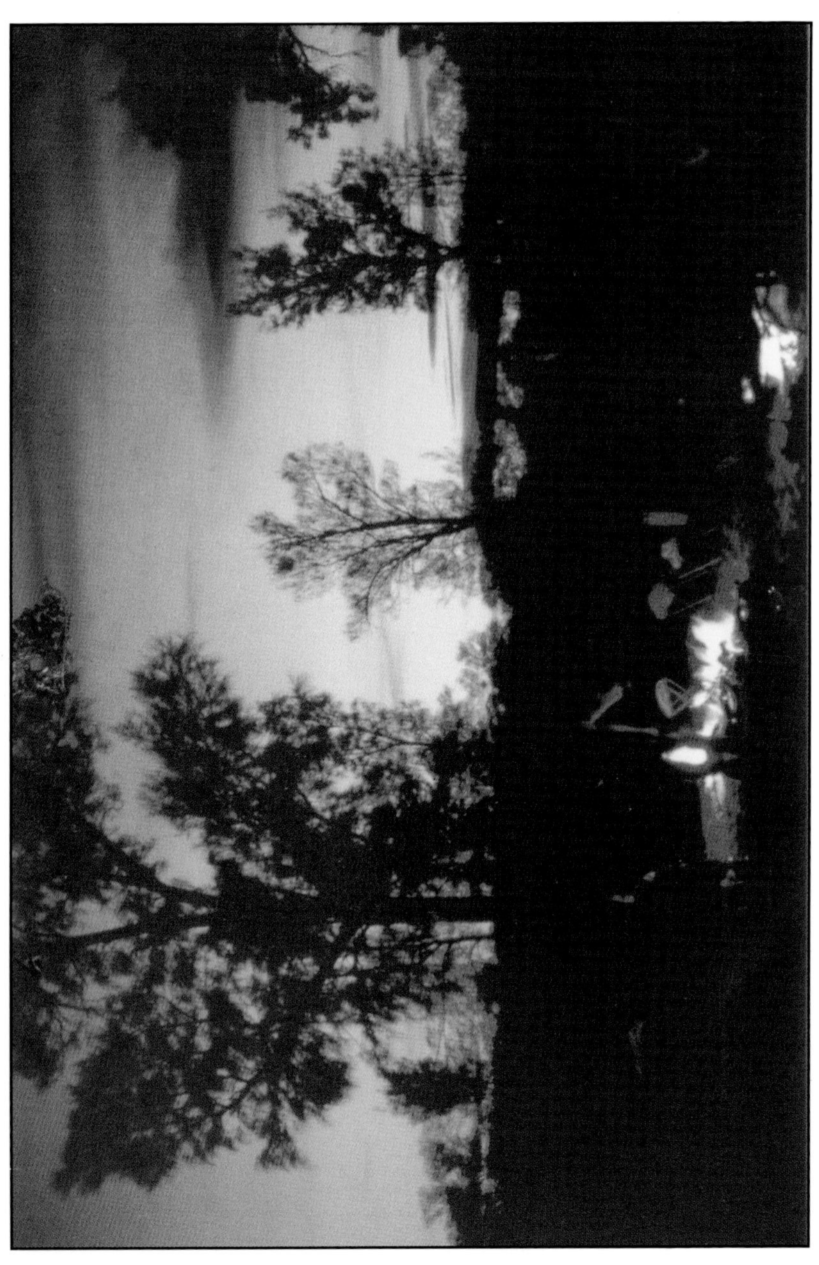

Anita Harper's sunset

magnificent waterfall.

Willy Oenpelli was always the fire lighter. On this occasion he asked Harry if he had a match. If he didn't have a match Willy would have got out his firesticks: one soft wood fire stick with little nicked dentations in it. Then he would place the end of a hard wood fire stick in the nicked dentation and twirl it with both hands. Beneath the soft fire stick he placed some dry grass or pandanus leaves, and the rubbing of the hard wood stick on the soft wood stick created smouldering dust to fall on the dry grass. Hey presto – a fire.

What could be better than to sit around a campfire in the moonlight at Beswick Lagoon listening to Rolf singing some of his more appropriate songs for the present company? He and Harry Butler wrote the following on another occasion when he was in the company of Blanasi and friend, when Blanasi accompanied him with his didgeridoo:

*Sun Arise she bring in the morning*
*Sun Arise bring in the morning*
*Fluttering her skirts all around*
*Sun Arise come with the dawning*
*Sun Arise she come every day*
*Sun Arise bring in the morning*
*Sun Arise every every every every day*
*She drive away the darkness every day*

*Drive away the darkness*
*Bringing back the warmth to the ground*
*Sun Arise oh oh sun arise oh oh*
*Spreading all the light all around*

"Sun Arise" became a hit record for Rolf.

Rolf is a born entertainer. You just can't stop him singing. I came across him on his own in the bush entertaining himself. There he was patting himself on his head and beating time with both his hands, as he made up a new tune.

Not only the Aboriginals enjoyed this impromptu concert in the bush, both Harry and I were very privileged to be there.

All slept soundly that night under a million stars.

Thousands of white screeching cockatoos, along with a magnificent chorus of singing honeyeaters in the Pandanus Palms above gave us a delightful awakening.

The birds did not wake the three Aboriginal men, they were up before the Piccaninny Dawn and had already speared a bucketful of fish to be cooked on the coals of our campfire for breakfast. One of the buckets only had one fish in it, as it was a small Barramundi, well I mean small by Northern Territory standards, it was about 3 kilos.

"There you see Rolf, you won't want all those tins of baked beans after all," I advised jokingly.

Left Hand Paddy scooped a hole in the sandy beach

about 1 metre long 30 centimetres wide and 60 centimetres deep. He then placed several fist-sized rocks in the hole and lit a fire on top of the rocks with one of Harry's matches. We all watched with interest as half an hour later, he hooked the rocks out and lined the bottom of the hole with wattle tree leaves. The Barramundi was still kicking as he laid it on the wattle leaves; he then covered it with more leaves and finally filled the hole completely with beach sand.

Fifty-five minutes later Willy seemed to take charge and said, "No Paddy no take the fish out yet, more, more time cook." It was about two minutes later; Willy scooped the sand carefully off the top layer of wattle leaves, and very carefully uncovered the cooked fish. Taking his knife from his belt he cut the fish scales just behind its gill, then peeled the skin back, scales and all, the full length to expose the mouth-watering sizzling juicy side of the Barramundi. The other fish were cooked directly on the coals. What a wonderful place to enjoy a wonderful breakfast.

We explored along the colourful cliff top as we made our way around the lagoon to the waterfall. The cliff top was very high above the water. It all could have ended there and then for me if luck hadn't been on my side.

Rolf and I were jumping from rock to rock trying to get into a good position to take photos of the waterfall at least 50 metres below us. I jumped onto a large rock near the edge of the cliff in order to get a better view over the edge of the cliff. Suddenly I felt a slight movement of the rock I was standing on, instinctively I jumped back onto a rock behind me. The large rock I had been standing on plunged 50 metres down on to the waterfall. Boy did I get a shock, and Rolf stood there white faced.

Whilst we explored the area and took many photographs, Blanasi and co were flat on their backs fast asleep in camp under the pandanus palms.

We travelled on deeper into Arnhemland, from each hill we climbed, the views offered a wider kaleidoscope of infinity.

"That's my country," Blanasi proudly exclaimed.

Some of the country we were now passing through was showing disturbing signs of having had late rains, with some parts of our track still covered with water and a few dangerous looking boggy patches. When you see water on the track, generally it is still OK to drive through; the ground is likely to be hard under the water. Once the water dries up and drains down into the soil that is when it is most likely to be a bog.

Yes the signs were there, and shortly after I made that observation we came to a bad looking patch on the track. I scouted the possibility of driving around the bog. No hope. Bad mushy ground all around.

"OK fellers you'll have to get out and walk a bit, as I try to ram through this lot," I said. "It's only 25 metres through so it should be OK."

I revved the motor after putting the vehicle into second high range, and let her go at the bog. The idea was to get up the traction before I hit the bog, easing off a little so I didn't spin the wheels, holding the steering straight as possible to keep the revolutions up. If you feel the vehicle losing way you have to drop down a gear real quick, hopefully you make it. Oh yes, I forgot to say, hold your breath while you do this.

At the end of the second day, we made short stops at two small settlements, Weemol and Bulman. As usual there were plenty more relatives to meet us. Another 17 kilometres and we arrived at the large Wilton River where we made our night camp once again under the Pandanus Palms.

The day had been extremely hot and humid and the sun was just going down, when Rolf ran from his tent in a lather of sweat, he ran to the river bank and dived in. He came to the surface about 20 metres out near midstream.

In his youth Rolf had been a junior champion swimmer. I watched from a distance at his flawless Australian crawl strokes as he glided along the river. I stood intrigued as I saw the Aboriginal boys running to the riverbank. I guessed they would be interested to learn that stroke. I knew they were all quite good swimmers.

Suddenly in an alarming voice Willy Oenpelli yelled, "Hey Rolf, there's a lot of crocodiles in that river." Rolf stopped dead in the water, and then swam at great speed to the bank, not stopping there. He broke the world record for 50 metres on dry land.

For the first time during the night we heard the disturbing sound of huge water buffaloes walking near our tents. The canvas of my tent seemed a lot thinner to me that night. The Wilton River is about 40 metres across, and it has a rocky bottom so it presents no problem at that time of the year. However during the wet season it is a raging torrent and impossible to cross on most days The Wilton has it's headwaters in what we call the stone country at the top of the escarpment in South–Western part of Arnhemland and it meanders down to join the mighty Roper River near the Roper Bar. We were now entering into one of the remotest regions of Australia travelling into the heart of Arnhemland. Our immediate destination was a small Aboriginal village called Ngaratj, where we would meet a number of Blanasi's relatives including his uncle. You might be surprised that I mention the word village. No doubt you've grown up being told that Aboriginals do not live in villages, they are nomads always on the move. WRONG. This has been taught in our schools since the beginning of time. This belief came about because most examples of Aboriginal life seen by white people, were the people of the desert country of Central Australia. They had to move on in order to find new sources of food, and follow the seasons for game such as kangaroos.

Those tribes living in more fertile country, such as Arnhemland, Cape York or the Kimberley stayed permanently for some years, before moving a short distance away to allow the heavily used land to recover.

I once met an old man who I judged to be over 80 years who told me that in his lifetime his tribe had moved to eight different locations along the river. In his old age he had come back to the village where he was born. Each move was about twenty kilometres. On arrival they would repair old bark houses their relatives lived in many years before. On all occasions the village was set well back away from the river.

Ngaratj was one of those villages. We still had a way to go, through some challenging flood prone land, where bogging was always possible.

The further we travelled into the heart, the fainter the wheel marks became.

At times Rolf and I had to take it in turns to walk out in front in order not to lose the track. Asking our native guides which way, drew the response, "Just drive that way" pointing north. We got somewhere sometime. About once or twice a year a vehicle would traverse this country packed with black bodies going from either Maningrida to Beswick or Bamyili or vice versa.

Blanasi and I were standing on the platform on the tail of the vehicle (we all loved to ride out there as it was better than being in the crowded seats inboard). Rolf was driving slowly through heavy scrub following the faint tracks. I could hear Harry entertaining Rolf singing at the top of his voice, his old shearing shed songs that Rolf loved.

Often when those two were in the front they both sang at the top of their voices. One song they both sang together often was.

*She'll be coming round the*
*mountain when she comes.*
*She'll be coming round the*
*mountain when she comes*
*She'll be coming round the mountain*
*Coming round the mountain*
*She'll be coming round the*
*mountain when she comes*

In the middle of that racket I heard Willy's voice call out to us from his back seat.

"Blanasi and Bert we are just about to pass a great big buffalo."

Standing on the back platform, we both watched anxiously as Rolf, still singing loudly, negotiated around the bull buffalo who was shaking his head wildly with those huge dangerous horns threatening close to our vehicle. He wasn't about to move for the intruders. Both Blanasi and I breathed a sigh a relief as we passed the beast.

All of a sudden Blanasi yelled at the top of his voice, "B-B-BERT HIM BLOODY BUFFALO HIM CHASIN' US CLOSE UP QUICK"

I swung my head over the side of the vehicle to call out to Rolf who was still singing.

"Rolf for Christ sake get going, the bloody buffalo is charging us."

I saw the back of Rolf's head poke out of the door window. He shouted, "What you say, you want to stop?"

We two yelled, in union (me in English, Blanasi in Rembarrngna.) "Not stop, get to hell out of here the buffalo is charging us." Thanks to the rainbow serpent, Rolf heard us and jammed down on the accelerator with the bull just two metres away. By this time Blanasi was up on top of the canvas roof with his feet in Willy's face.

The three Aboriginals had been through this country on foot a number of times during their lives. However they never quite knew where they were at any given time. When they travel they have no particular arrival time. We get there some time.

Half way down a rocky hill we came across a beautiful water spring and pool. After replenishing our water containers. We all jumped into that beautiful cool water. As usual the weather was hot and humid. Harry, Rolf and I stayed in for an hour just floating and dog paddling around. The other three only spent a few minutes in the water before getting out and lying in the sun.

"Him too cold for blackfella," Blanasi remarked.

Continuing late in the afternoon when it was cooler, we covered another 20 kilometres before we stopped at a small stream to camp. Although the stream was only about three metres wide and three or four metres deep, Willy went to work with his fishing spear.

His spear was four pronged and in his hands it was quite an efficient tool for fishing. I didn't think he would catch anything in such a small shallow creek. I was surprised when he arrived back with two dozen large sized fresh water shrimps and two long necked tortoises, and four dozen (large as your hand) freshwater mussels.

At dinner that evening we enjoyed Hors d'Oeuvres before tucking into Harry's Tinned Tomato soup and Rice Flap Jacks.

Our journey continued along the imagined track. Sometimes we could not see it unless one of us walked in front, this made progress very slow.

Willy and Rolf were riding on the platform at the back, as Harry took his turn to drive. None of the Aboriginals could drive. We were travelling through some spectacular country featuring most unusually shaped termite nests. Rolf spent a lot of time stopping us and taking many photos.

These termite nests, or as they are sometimes called Anthills, were Magnetic termite nests. These little fellows built their mounds lengthwise always facing north–south. The sides stretched out to about 40 centimetres each side of centre at the bottom, then shaped to a sharp edge along the top for the full length of the mound. These clever little termites thus created a system of air-conditioning for their home. The sun coming up in the east in the morning is at its lowest temperature impacting on the broadsides. During the suns hottest time at midday, it is directly overhead. Therefore its impact on the thin edge at the top of the mound has less area to heat the mound.

"We bin close up uncles place now," Blanasi said. Willy pointed to a large sharply pointed rocky hill, "Him just near him hill." I judged it to be about two kilometres away. We crossed another creek, that I found out later was the headwaters of the Cadell River. Soon we could hear dogs barking as they advertised our arrival.

Blanasi instructed us to stop about three hundred metres from the circular cluster of bark houses we could see in the distance.

"Why are we stopping here?" Harry enquired of Blanasi.

"Me go walkin' in first," he explained. I had been here before on a number of occasions with my friend, so I explained to Rolf and Harry, that they were witnessing the protocol of old tribal behaviour. "Remember, these people still live today in 1973, as they and their ancestors lived for thousands of years." I went on. "Just keep your eyes on Blanasi."

All the bark houses were in a very large circle; I suppose the circle would have had a diameter of two hundred metres. In the middle of that circle, was a round ring of stones circling a smouldering fire. Also directly in front of the little bark houses that are built up on stilts, were circles of stones around fires expelling thin spiralling whiffs of blue smoke. Families could be seen sitting cross-legged on the ground around these small household fires. The one thing that Harry and Rolf were quick to notice was that as Blanasi walked casually into the large circle, his eyes appeared to be looking at his feet. Not one person acknowledged his presence. Many children could be seen playing nearby. They also ignored the visitor. On arriving at the large ring of stones he sat down cross-legged with his head bode. We visitors waited in anticipation of the next move. There a stately tall old man stood up from his position in front of his bark house and casually walked towards the visitor. He also walked slowly with his head bode. When he arrived at the centre circle he stopped a few metres from Blanasi. He did not appear to speak. Blanasi casually stood up and turned to face the old man.

At that moment both smiled and embraced. Willy, who hadn't said a word since Blanasi departed said, "Him Blanasi now tell uncle we here." At that moment Blanasi was seen to point in our direction. Now all the children ran yelling and jumping towards the visitor, many other families could be seen making their way to the centre circle to welcome their relation.

We waited for half an hour. Blanasi came back and said, “Uncle say. Come on to a place, I will show you where to make camp. We drove under instructions to within one hundred metres on the edge where there were no houses and stopped.

We unpacked and put up our tents for the first time on this trip. This was also under Blanasi’s instructions. He explained we do not sleep in open here.

Willy performed his usual duty by gathering firewood and starting a fire. We had only just sat down on the stools we carried, but had never used before, when we noticed two girls about 14 or 15 years of age coming towards our camp smiling, each girl carried something wrapped in a bundle of paperbark. They laid it down at Blanasi’s feet, and without saying a single word, they smiled again and returned to the circle of bark houses from whence they came.

With a wave of his hand to us Blanasi indicated to sit down around the fire.

Carefully unwrapping the parcel, we were all delighted at the gift from the villagers to us visitors. More deliciously freshly cooked fish than we could hope to eat.

We had finished our wonderful meal and a cup of

tea, when Blanasi advised us, "Uncle him come now." We all stood up as the straight standing old man approached smiling. "Uncle these blokes my friends, This one you know." He pointed to me. I stepped forward and shook Uncles hand. "Dis one him Rolf, an Dis big fella Harry him cook up tucker."

Uncle then turned his attention to Willy Oenpelli, and Left Hand Paddy, whom he obviously knew.

Uncle then spoke to Blanasi in their native tongue. With a wave of his hand he turned and with slow long strides walked back to his family's house.

Of course we were all so pleased to meet Uncle. Rolf especially, as he knew that Uncle was one of the greatest X-ray bark painters in the world.

A famous Professor on an exploration journey through Arnhemland discovered Uncle Mandarg as a young man in 1948.

Consequently Mandarg's name became synonymous worldwide for his x-ray bark paintings.

What a wonderful stay of three days, to live the life of the tribal Aboriginals, in the style that we probably will never experience again.

During the afternoon, Rolf entertained the shy little children. With his skill, he soon had them singing and clowning around. He pulled funny faces, barked at the camp dogs, did tricks with his hands making a 2 cent coin disappear.

That evening just before the sun went down, Uncle Mandarg invited us to go with him down to the river to see how he caught all those tasty fish we had for dinner last night.

For thousands of years Mandarg's ancestors have been catching fish in the same place. At the spot where he sat us down on the bank a two metre deep creek divided into two separate channels, each about two metres wide. He then showed us a bark wall about three metres long fixed to a long pole that was hanging across and above one of the creek channels.

We were then required to walk with him about two hundred metres down stream. There our delightful host showed us the business end of his fishing apparatus.

Built at the two separate channels were two races built with short 2cm thick branches laid across corduroy fashion making a bridge like structure. With a little branch fence along the channel on both sides running barely under water for about 30 metres. The entrance to the race was deep in the water, with the race gradually rising higher up in the river making the water shallower every few metres. At the end of the race was placed a large basket made from pandanus fonds.

The reason behind the operation is that in the natural state, when the tide is going out in the river the fish swim down stream so as not to get caught high and dry.

Hence Mandarg has the bark wall to divert the river

water away from the channel he has set the basket. The water in that channel recedes and the fish think that the tide is going out so they swim like heck along the very shallow race and into the basket thank you. Plenty of fresh water mullet and Long Toms small Barramundi, Saratoga and Rifle Fish.

As Mandarg set his bark wall, we all watched in anticipation. Suddenly there flapping and wriggling their way along the race came a stream of bewildered fish into a basket with all their mates.

The moon was bright as we all sat at the communal fireplace in the centre of the large circle. Some of the children with Mandarg's encouragement, danced to the tune of Blanasi and his didgeridoo. Rolf hypnotised or put some to sleep when he quietly sang

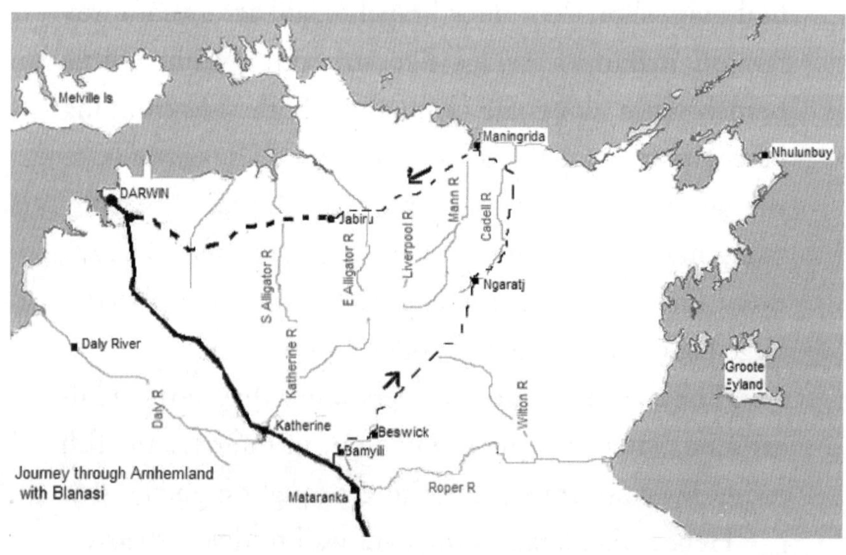

*There's a lake in North Australia*
*Little lake with lovely name*
*And the story woven round it*
*All the little children came*
*Every night the native mothers*
*Sing this lovely lullaby*
*Songs across the moonlight waters*
*To the stars up in the sky.*

We made our sad departure from Ngaratj and although I didn't know, I was willing to bet that Mandarg was responsible for lining all the happy families of Ngaratj along the track waving to us as we drove by, heading to the large Aboriginal settlement on the coast of the Arafura Sea, Manangrida.

It was one of the largest settlements on the north coast. It had a population of approximately 400 families, not including the large number of relatives visiting from other areas at any given time. These people often built temporary shacks on the outskirts of town. The permanent families live in normal cottages with backyards and in some cases gardens. Most of the streets were paved and had streetlights. There was a large school and pre school, with married teacher houses, single teacher units, and a number of other government buildings, and offices. The general store stocked most food, items of clothing, tools and hardware supplies. The sports oval and playground included a swimming pool and basketball court. There was a piped water supply and sewage system provided throughout the town area. Maningrida was quite a live-able modern little town. Our observations indicated that the inhabitants were a happy lot.

As usual our three Aboriginal friends had plenty of relatives and friends to stay with or visit. Rolf went off and made official visits to important people such as the settlement Manager, Department of Aboriginal Affairs Officers, and school teachers. Harry and I spent most of our one-day stop, attending to maintenance of our Nissan that served us without problems on this rugged journey.

Our first obstacle after departing Maningrida was crossing the massive Liverpool River that is enlarged by joining with the huge Mann River just a few kilometres up stream to form an impossible barrier in the wet season. Fortunately in the month of May most of the flood-waters of the wet season had subsided, and we found only shallow water crossings at the numerous rivers and creeks we encountered, until we reached the border of Arnhemland. The East Alligator River is the forbidden barrier to uninvited guests or non-permit holders.

You may be mystified as to the name of this river. We do not have alligators in Australia. We have crocodiles. This name came about when in the 1800s a British ship was exploring the Northern Coast of Australia and the sailors saw crocodiles.

They mistook these massive creatures for alligators.

The track we had travelled on from Maningrida was a well-used roadway, which was periodically graded by Aboriginal road workers throughout the dry season.

Crossing the East Alligator River on the cement forge, we entered land which today is one of the world treasures, Kakadu National Park, featuring hard top roads, motels, and shopping centres. Unfortunately dangerously close to the National Park is one of the world's largest uranium mines.

Kakadu National Park is by far Australia's biggest national park, covering very diverse country from the Ancient Arnhemland Escarpment to the wonderful wetlands of the flood plains. An area of over 20,000 square kilometres. It's natural geological features, include rock formations, spectacular waterfalls, thousands of water birds on the many lagoons, as well as an extensive wildlife list.

Many warning notices advertise that the dangerous estuarine (salt water) crocodiles are present in and near the waterways.

Featured also is probably the finest display of Aboriginal Rock art in the hundreds of caves with impressive evidence of great age.

With just 147 kilometres to Darwin on a made road, at last our small group of friends could fit inside our vehicle, as we had eaten all the boxes of food we carried on part of the back seat.

As we drove, all were sadly reflecting the end in silence. I thought we shouldn't be feeling so sad. It had been a wonderful joyous three weeks with six good friends having a wonderful time together.

Shortly after, we arrived at the Darwin airport and said goodbye to Rolf.

Driving down the highway back to Bamyili, to return our friends to their families, I reflected on memories gone by.

I have many great memories of Blanasi performances. One especially stands out. We had toured New Zealand for ten days doing concerts in the cities and some large towns. At each venue Blanasi had been front-page news in all the papers. On our return flight to Sydney a hostess came to me and said, "Many passengers have asked me to ask Mr Blanasi if he would play his didgeridoo for the passengers."

I replied, "You had better ask Mr Blanasi."

Which she did. With a broad smile he said, "Sure I do dat." He stood up and taking his instrument from the locker above, he began playing as he walked up and down every aisle of the jumbo jet. For a full ten minutes he went through his repertoire, even playing the birds song and dingo call.

I have never heard such a roar of approval and clapping in a plane after the conclusion of his airborne performance. I am certain I never will again.

Blanasi take a bow. Bor Bor my friend.

Fish trap

# *The Great Journey North*

Matthew Dillon Cox was relaxing on a pure silk mattress on his hammock slung between two magnificent old palm trees. The tropical sea breeze gently blowing in from the deep blue waters of the Java Sea. The newspaper he had been reading lay on his chest. He reached to the swinging table to clasp a cool glass of scotch and dry. Every few minutes a beautiful island girl, with a frangipani in her hair and wearing a colourful sarong, would pass by to render any request to the master. Life was great for Dillon Cox. He certainly appreciated the huge fortune he had made in Bendigo, Bathurst and Hill End as a gold buyer.

However as he lay in comfort he contemplated his life now as compared to twenty years ago. He left school early to assist his widowed mother in bringing up four young children alone. Her husband and the father of the children, had been killed in a mining accident on the Victorian Goldfields in Bendigo. Acting against his mother's wishes young Dillon worked underground, often in very dangerous positions. However, the money was good and besides helping his mother he diligently saved and invested his money in new goldmines going into production. With judgments belying his age, his investments proved so profitable that he turned to buying gold. Cox soon became a household name with gold-buying offices all over Victoria and New South Wales. As time went by his mother passed away, and his brothers and sisters went their separate ways. Cox, now a very wealthy man, decided to retire to a warmer climate and the pleasant lifestyle at Batavia, Jakarta on the island of Java, where he built a mansion.

The Australian newspaper he had been reading stirred his imagination with the headlines.

GOLD FOUND IN THE
NORTHERN TERRITORY.
PINE CREEK THE CENTRE OF A GOLD RUSH.

The temptation was too great. Dillon Cox immediately boarded the steamship Marie Elizabeth to travel the several hundred kilometres across the Java Sea to Darwin. His first stop in Darwin was the mining registry office where he registered as a gold buyer. He then secured an office and opened for business. He was fortunate that no other gold buyer was yet established in Darwin. Consequently he was in a position to purchase gold from the desperate miners at a very favourable price. Dillon Cox also found that there was a great shortage of meat for the hungry goldminers. Being the shrewd businessman, he employed an accountant to operate his gold buying office, and then caught a sailing ship to Rockhampton in Queensland and bought 500 head of store cattle at a property on the Burdekin River.

His plan was to overland the cattle to Darwin, slaughter them and sell meat to the miners. All station owners and drovers around Rockhampton laughed at the suggestion of anyone stupid enough to suggest droving cattle through 3200 kilometres of unexplored and wild outback country to Darwin. Only an ignorant city businessman would suggest such an impossibility. The Rockhampton newspapers even printed the story for a laugh.

Walking down the street from the auctioneer's office where Dillon Cox had paid for the cattle he wondered, *had he made a mistake?* He was a little worried. A tap on his shoulder startled him and he swung around to confront a young man of about 22 years of age. With a confident broad smile the young man said, "Mr Cox, I will deliver your cattle all the way to Darwin and I would hope not to lose any on the way." Dillon Cox observed this big strong young man. He spoke with an Irish accent.

"What is your name?" Cox enquired.

"My name is Wentworth D'Arcy Uhr Sir."

This young Irishman had arrived in Brisbane in 1860. He spent four months looking at various job prospects and eventually he chose to join the Queensland Mounted Police. His first assignment was to join Victorian explorer William Landsborough who was to be sent by the Government in search of the missing Burke & Wills expedition. With equipment for the search and four horses they were shipped to the Gulf of Carpentaria. On arrival they sailed up the Albert River as far as possible, made a base camp, then set about their search for any sign of the missing explorers. Although they were in the region where the explorers had travelled six months before, the heavy tropical rains of the Northern wet season had obliterated their tracks. On Christmas Day 1861 the two men had searched several hundred kilometres inland from their base on the Albert River. Landsborough and Uhr spent the day resting at the spot where the town of Camooweal stands today on the banks of the Georgina River. History tells us that on that Christmas Day 1861, both Burke and Wills lay dead at Cooper Creek. At that point with no sign of the missing men, Landsborough decided to return to Brisbane through unexplored country – a distance of over 1600 kilometres.

On that journey Landsborough and Uhr discovered the wonderful grazing lands of the Queensland channel country. On arrival back in Brisbane D'Arcy Uhr resigned from the Queensland Mounted Police. He liked what he had seen of the outback.

He then spent several years working on cattle stations and working as a drover. Six years after Uhr had taken the first mob of cattle to the Northern Territory, the great cattle drives to the North began. Burketown was established at the spot where Landsborough and Uhr had made their base camp. Burketown soon became the supply centre for the thousands of cattle and their drovers passing that way, and it had a population of over five thousand. To cater for the hundreds of drovers and other travellers many hotels and gambling houses were established. At this time in history the New South Wales and Victorian Police were arresting and convicting many of the notorious Bush Rangers who had been such a problem in the southern states.

Many of these villains were heading north in search of new places to operate their illegal lifestyle. With all the gambling and bawdy houses, Burketown was the perfect setting for the villains from the South. Lawlessness was rife. The Queensland Government, in an attempt to stop the lawlessness, appointed the now Magistrate William Landsborough to the position to establish law and order in Burketown. Once again Landsborough chose

Wentworth D'Arcy Uhr as his bodyguard. Uhr rejoined the Queensland Mounted Police and became the Lawman of the Gulf country.

The period of the great cattle drives to the north of Australia were very similar to the Westward Ho wagon trains on the Oregon or Santa Fe trails and just as dangerous. However, the opposition who fought to protect their land were the Aborigines, while the Americans fought the Red Indians. In Northern Australia, as in the Wild West of America, the drovers and stockmen all carried six guns in their holsters and they were quick on the draw and as straight a shot as the Sundance Kid. Apart from being quick D'Arcy Uhr was an excellent horse rider and an expert with a long stock whip. That was the scene confronting Landsborough and Uhr on arrival at Burketown in 1885.

Almost daily, gunfights occurred in the main street. On one occasion Uhr happened to be walking past one of the hotel gambling houses when through the swinging doors tumbled two men fist fighting. One man was knocked to the ground and he drew his six-gun. As he took aim at his opponent, Uhr's stock whip curled around the barrel of that six shooter, and it was pulled from the would-be shooter's hand.

On another occasion two men robbed a gambling house of their cash and ran from the building, stealing two riding horses and ten packhorses. They then galloped out of town heading south. A few miles south of Burketown, Uhr was riding on the same track heading towards town when he and the two robbers waved greetings as they rode past each other. By the time Uhr arrived back in town and learnt of the robbery he had to organise several packhorses and food before he could depart in pursuit of the bandits. By this time the bandits had a five hour start on the lawman, which translated into about 120 kilometres – a huge start to give horsemen.

Uhr travelled all night trying to make up time. As he rode he followed the horse tracks of the bandits, which he could separate from other horsemen's tracks by a partly broken horseshoe of one of their horses.

This chase now became one of the longest pursuits in history. Uhr continued his chase for more than 1600 kilometres. He eventually caught up with the two men on the Castlereagh track, New South Wales, and after a fierce gunfight the robbers threw down their guns and surrendered. He was then required to escort them back to Queensland to face trial. Two months later he was back in Burketown reporting to his boss William Landsborough.

Wentworth D'Arcy Uhr is in the history books for being the first drover to deliver 500 head of cattle to his relieved partner Matthew Dillon Cox. From his experiences in the Gulf country as a mounted policeman,

D'Arcy Uhr had studied the route taken by Leichhardt on his exploration journey to Port Essington in 1845. His first move was to engage four drovers to assist him with the difficult task.

From Leichhardt's report he was aware that the strong Kalkadoon tribesmen of the Gulf country could attack him. With this knowledge he planned his defence in advance. Each day one of his men would ride several miles ahead of the cattle, looking for any signs of the presence of wild natives in the area. The two ringers riding separately around the cattle each night were in position to offer warning of an attack. At times grass fires were started by the natives to hinder their progress. On those occasions the advance riders were in a position to warn the drovers to halt the cattle before the burnt area was reached.

Leichhardt's information on the position and size of the rivers also assisted the drovers to plan their course. On reaching the Roper River, instead of crossing Leichhardt's Roper Bar into the rugged country Leichhardt had described (today known as Arnhem land) they followed on the south side of the Roper all the way until they reached the Katherine River. From there to Cox's new station they experienced no problems.

As the cattle were on their four month trek north, Dillon Cox was busy leasing the land that later was to become his cattle station. This land is today known as

Cox's Peninsula on the western side of the Darwin harbour in the Northern Territory.

The success of Wentworth D'Arcy Uhr's journey with Dillon Cox's cattle brought him many offers of droving great mobs of cattle to the Northern Territory.

When John McCartney established Florida Cattle Station on the Goyder River in the land today known as Arnhem land he claimed 19,000 square kilometres of country – the world's largest cattle station. Wentworth D'Arcy Uhr was given the responsibility of delivering 5000 head of cattle from St George region of Queensland to Florida Station. On this occasion he was not required to "blaze a new track". He followed the Castlereagh track used by the hundreds of prospector miners from the Victorian and New South Wales goldfields when they had headed for the Pine Creek goldfields. On arrival at Florida Station, D'Arcy Uhr was given the unenviable task of manager. John McCartney had given him a staff of approximately fifteen including stockmen, a blacksmith, Chinese cook and Chinese gardeners. Soon it was clear they would face tremendous problems.

Almost daily the fierce tribal Aborigines attacked the white men. Several Chinese gardeners were speared to death working in the vegetable gardens. Hundreds of cattle were speared, providing very easy food for the tribal people of the region. Even with guns as defence the natives won the battle by sheer numbers. After four desperate years John McCartney moved out of the tribal lands with a very small number of the five thousand cattle he had taken into Florida. D'Arcy Uhr got the job of droving the remaining cattle 1200 kilometres to the western side of the Northern Territory to form Auvergne station on the Baines River. After the experience D'Arcy Uhr had managing the Florida cattle station he turned down the offer made to him by John McCartney to manage Auvergne Station.

For a change he decided to do a little exploring for new grazing country. In this venture he and Jock McPhee explored the Victoria River. To look the country over on the northern side of the river they had to brave the dangers of crocodiles by crossing the river in a native dug out canoe. Moving further east to the Roper River they followed it to the mouth, riding south once more, to the headwaters of the MacArthur River. With the help of a native boy they had befriended along the way, they travelled the length of the MacArthur River in a canoe and the native boy followed with their horses. About this time gold at the Pine Creek field had been worked out and a new gold rush had begun with the miners moving out to the new finds.

Gold by the bucketful was being picked up in the dry bed of the Palmer River in Cape York. Hundreds of miners were making their way to the new fields. Some who had been lucky finding gold at Pine Creek travelled in wagonettes, while others travelled by horse and cart, or rode their horse with their swag strapped to the back of the saddle. If their luck had been out they had to walk, pushing their wheelbarrows the 1700 kilometres to the Palmer River. One other group, also at Pine Creek when the gold had finished, were two thousand Chinese trying to eke out an existence. The ruthless landlords of China had shipped these poor unfortunate people overseas from their homeland and families.

They came with promises of great riches if they found gold and sent it back to the landlords. However, they were never given the opportunity to return home and often their families were murdered.

How were they to find their way to far off Palmer River goldfields? Our good friend Wentworth D'Arcy Uhr offered to help, and began probably the most bizarre droving fete in the history of the world.

For the price of a piece of gold the size of a little finger, he would deliver them to the Palmer River goldfields. Yes, just imagine two thousand little fingers of gold. The long line of Chinamen walked carrying all their rice and belongings in baskets hanging from yokes across their shoulders.

Wentworth D'Arcy Uhr, on his beautiful white stallion with stock whip in hand, continually rode around the strung-out walkers just like droving cattle. At times

he cracked his stock whip at the tailenders when they lagged behind. Crossing some of the large rivers in the Gulf country presented a problem as some of the tail-enders were taken by crocodiles. However, they had paid their fare and there would be no refund. Another problem the drover was unable to solve was that when D'Arcy Uhr was at the head of the group the wild Kalkadoon tribesmen would attack the tailenders, and subsequently several Chinamen disappeared.

After three months most of the Chinese gold prospectors arrived at Palmer River. For several years after Uhr took many large mobs of cattle to the Northern Territory and the Kimberley to establish many new cattle stations.

After the first droving feats of D'Arcy Uhr, thousands of cattle and drovers followed his well-worn tracks from New South Wales and Queensland into the northern regions. They included the Durack Brothers – Big Johnnie and Long Michael, and the MacDonald brothers, Willie and Charlie. They were on the track for two years travelling 4000 kilometres from the Goulburn district to the Fitzroy and Margaret River junction in the Kimberley. The Duracks began their cattle drive from Kyabra Creek near Cooper Creek in Western Queensland with 7520 cattle split into four different mobs travelling separately, along with 200 horses and four covered wagons with supplies. They travelled via the

Diamantina and Georgina Rivers before picking up supplies at Burketown and joining D'Arcy Uhr's track to the outpost store at Borroloola and Leichhardt's crossing at Roper Bar. At that point they had been on the drive for twelve months. When they arrived at their destination at the Ord River in the Kimberley, their journey had taken 18 months.

Other great names to follow Uhr's track were Nat Buchanan, brothers Hugh and Wattie Gordon, and "Greenhide" Sam Croker. Many others, too numerous to mention, followed. One of the favourite camps to rest their cattle was "at the Currie" Cloncurry. The river there always had good grazing along the banks and was never dry. Also never dry was the bar at The Drovers Rest Hotel. At "the Currie", late at night or early morn, one would often hear Irish voices singing this old ballad about drovers making camp and resting cattle on other people's grass:

*When the overlanders gather*
*In the wide and dusty plain*
*And they never speak of rain*
*When the blazing sun is setting*
*When tomorrow is never mentioned*
*Like a disc of shining brass*
*They wouldn't steal a copper*
*But they all steal grass*

At this time in the history of droving, all drovers had to take the route via Katherine and on to the Victoria River if they were heading for the Kimberley. It was years before Nat "Bluey" Buchanan fought his way across the long dry stage to form the Murranji track. With many of the Kimberley cattle stations now established there were many people looking for land for cattle stations. In an effort to find new pastures Nat Buchanan, John Costello, "Greenhide" Sam Croker and D'Arcy Uhr set out across unexplored country to the West Kimberley coast. They looked over the country around the Prince Regent and Glenelg Rivers, however, the remoteness of the area proved unpopular, so that area was never settled. Today most of the Prince Regent River region is utilised as a National Park.

Few stories have been written of the exploits of Wentworth D'Arcy Uhr. The ever exciting cry "Gold!" once again set the hopeful miners travelling to new country. This time it was to the far off Kimberley of Western Australia. Gold was discovered at Halls Creek in 1886. D'Arcy Uhr in partnership with Nat Buchanan and Jock McPhee decided that rather than dig for gold, they could make more money selling meat to the miners. So they set up a slaughter yard and butcher shop. Nat Buchanan and Jock McPhee brought the cattle over from Queensland, now on the shortened route via Nat "Bluey" Buchanan's Murranji Track, to the slaughter yards. D'Arcy Uhr man-

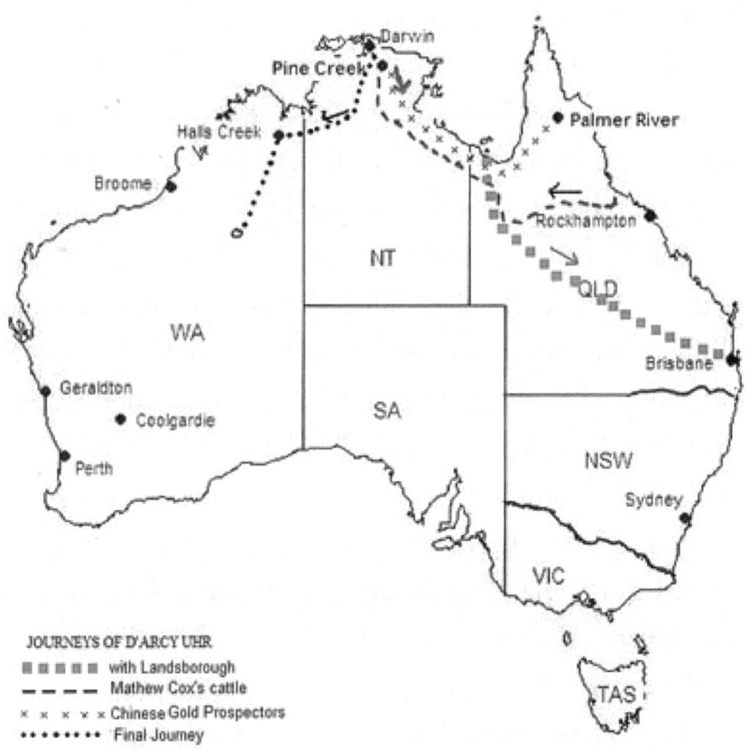


aged the slaughter yard and butcher shop and he also set up a gold-buying office in Halls Creek with all the money he had from all those little fingers of the Chinese.

He was soon flushed with money and after a little over a year all the gold at Halls Creek was gone. Throughout the history of this country the miners have moved on to the next gold rush when the gold has run out. Halls Creek, however, is still a cattle country town.

The next destination for gold was far away at Coolgardie, 5000 kilometres to the south. Once again the wagons, the carts, the horse riders, and the walkers travelled deserted tracks to the Western Australian coast. Bypassing the pearling centre of the world, Broome, they continued south to the point where Geraldton stands today. They then moved south-east into dangerous wild Aboriginal country, eventually arriving at the booming township of Coolgardie. D'Arcy Uhr studied the inadequate map of the country to find the shortest possible way direct to Coolgardie. He would be at Coolgardie long before all the others, travelling the long way around. Wentworth D'Arcy Uhr set off with his beautiful white stallion and two packhorses loaded with food. In his saddlebags he carried all the money from all those fingers. As well he carried many bars of pure gold, the takings of the last gold of Halls Creek. He headed into the desert which today marks the Canning Stock Route. Our hero Wentworth D'Arcy Uhr was never seen again. Somewhere in the sand hills of the Great Sandy Desert lay two saddlebags of money and gold.

# *Daisy Bates, Kabbarli (Dreamtime Grandmother)*

In 1861 the Gregory Brothers set out from Perth on an expedition to explore the north-west coast of Western Australia, seeking out new grazing lands for development. Whilst travelling along the coast, where Roebourne is today, they discovered quantities of 'mother of pearl' shell with some of the shells even containing precious pearls. It was further investigated and eventually a pearling industry was established in the north-west and Broome became the centre for the new industry.

Pearl shell was found for several hundred kilometres from Shark Bay to the Kimberley coast. By the mid

1890s Broome had become the world centre for the selling and buying of mother of pearl shell, which was mainly used for buttons in the clothing industry.

Precious pearls brought high prices from jewellers overseas. The port became the home for hundreds of pearling luggers seeking pearl shell along the coast.

The masters of the luggers were mainly Europeans and the crews a mixture of Asians. Most of the divers were Japanese or Malaysian. Men from China and the Philippines were also employed in the industry. It was the usual for the luggers to put to sea on the Monday morning and return to Broome on the following Friday afternoon with their cargo of pearl shell. On arrival the lugger crews would load the bags onto trolleys then push the trolleys on rail tracks into large sheds where auctions would take place at a later date. The crews would then be free to take leave for the weekend.

Money flowed freely and the five hotels were doing brisk business. Gambling and drunkenness were rife. At these times some sporting contests were organised for the crews.

One of the most popular sporting contests was rifle shooting. The teams representing the various luggers would travel out into the bush to the east of Broome to see which team could bag the most trophies. They would shoot kangaroos, emus, dingoes and any bush Aborigines they came across – men, women or children. To prove their success they were required to cut off an ear and return with it in order to claim a team victory.

At the same time the crew members would capture the most desirable young women and take them back to their lugger. Then they would take them to sea for that week, to indulge their sordid sexual pleasures.

Still worse was to follow and it is hard to conceive the cruelty of some human beings. Often on their return journey back to Broome on the Friday afternoon they would have tired of these unfortunate females, so they would throw them overboard to drown or be taken by sharks. Eventually these dreadful activities became known in the capital city of Perth and were brought to the notice of members in Parliament. However the government minister responsible took no action. He took the view that those hard working crewmen, in a very remote place, and under very poor conditions, needed some form of relaxation.

He stated that, "The crew members are doing no harm by killing a few useless wild savages."

Eventually the stories of these atrocities began appearing in the newspapers in New York, London and Paris. They created such public interest and outcry that the London Times decided to send one of their most brilliant journalists all the way to Fremantle, and then on to Broome to check that the stories were not just rumours.

Daisy Bates was a young 28-year-old girl from Glen Carrick, Tipperary in Ireland. She had been well educated in the best school in Ireland before attending finishing schools in London and Paris. A few years before, when her name was Daisy O'Dwyer, she had travelled to Australia after advice from her doctor that she needed to go and live in a dryer, warmer climate. She arrived in Australia in 1884 with a pocket full of introductions. First she went to Tasmania to stay with family friends who lived among the landed gentry of the midlands in northern Tasmania. With their manor houses, English rose gardens, oak trees and apple orchards it was all a reminder of the old country.

Daisy O'Dwyer easily adapted to the local English lifestyle. She rode their beautiful thoroughbred horses at field picnics, and rode with the hounds at the local hounds' clubs of the upper class of Northern Tasmania. One year later Daisy O'Dwyer sailed to the mainland to continue her exciting new life. On arrival in Sydney she immediately enjoyed the company of many eligible sons of wealthy landowners from the South Coast of New South Wales. Soon after arriving in Sydney she met and fell in love with the son of a wealthy land-owning family of the South Coast. They were married in a small church in the village of Berry, situated just north of the town of Nowra. Her new husband's name was John Bates and in his company she was introduced to all the well-connected families of Sydney. John Bates, after marriage, failed to change his eligible bachelor lifestyle. He was often away from their home riding with the hounds or playing polo in Melbourne or Brisbane. This caused the marriage to fail. Daisy Bates then returned to London and established herself as a journalist of much repute.

Now, once more, she was packing her bags to sail back to Australia with the important assignment to confirm that these rumoured atrocities were true.

Soon after setting sail she met a Catholic priest, Father Martelli, and they became friends. Each day at sea they would spend time together as he taught her Italian. After a few weeks Daisy learnt that Father Martelli had been to Rome to report to the Pope on his missionary work in the Kimberley region of north-west Australia. After learning this information Daisy explained to her new friend that she was travelling to Fremantle, and then continuing on to Broome, to report on the conditions and lives of the Aboriginal people. During the next few weeks at sea, Father Martelli advised Daisy on the culture and customs of the Aborigines. He also taught her a few words of the Broome region's Aboriginal language.

On arrival in Fremantle, Daisy bought a horse and wagonette, camping and cooking equipment, and food supplies. She loaded this equipment on board the same sailing lugger Father Martelli was travelling on, and so was able to continue lessons. On arrival at Port Hedland,

Daisy and her wagonette

Daisy decided to leave the ship but not before she made a promise to Father Martelli that she would visit him at his Beagle Bay mission after she had completed her work in Broome.

Her first night in Port Hedland was the most restless and frightful of her life. Not only was she disturbed by drunken men swearing and fighting just outside her boarding house room, but her toes were nibbled by many hermit sand crabs running on the earthen floor.

Setting out from Port Hedland in her wagonette the very next day, with ample supplies of food and water, and even a few bags of chaff for her horse, she began her remarkable journey of 1200 kilomctres through unexplored country to Broome.

Along the way she met and befriended many Aboriginal people and learnt a lot of their culture and living conditions. Her journey took 6 months. Just imagine a woman on her own in 1886 travelling 1200 kilometres with a horse and wagonette through tropical heat and in country occupied only by bush Aborigines.

On arrival in Broome, Daisy set about investigating if the rumoured atrocities were really being committed. Her reports to her editor in London were so graphic and brilliantly written that they were syndicated to newspapers all over the world. The power of the pen of Daisy Bates proved so great that the Western Australian Government was forced to send troopers to Broome to stop the atrocities and to uphold the law in the town. Daisy is credited with saving countless lives through her writing for newspapers and to Government officials.

As promised, as she had finished her work in Broome, Daisy set off to visit Father Martelli at Beagle Bay mission. After seeing the dedication and devotion of Father Martelli she stayed to help her friend, working for and learning from the Aboriginal people. Daisy then decided to dedicate the rest of her life to the cause of helping the Aboriginal people cope with the changes to their lives after the arrival of European people in their country. She vowed never to preach white man religion to the native people, or change them in any way. She would help and advise them and assist with medical advice as best she could.

Thus began this remarkable woman's life in the bush with the Aborigines over the next 65 years.

At the turn of the century the opportunity to take up land in the north-west in order to develop cattle and sheep stations, was offered by the Government. Daisy availed herself of this offer with a plan to develop and operate a cattle station with the help, and for the benefit of, Aboriginal people. When granted a block of 5000 square kilometres of well-watered country near the head-waters of the Ashburton River, she travelled to Lake Eda station about 70 kilometres east of Broome and bought 770 head of well-bred Hereford cattle.

Next she engaged six stockmen as drovers, and a Maori cook, to assist her to drive the cattle to her new cattle station 1600 kms south. Travelling along the coast from Broome, via the eighty-mile beach, Daisy was soon confronted with problems.

The stockmen proved very inexperienced and the Maori cook had to be dismissed as unsuitable for the task of providing reasonable meals for the group. Four months after leaving Broome, they arrived at Marble Bar, where Daisy rested her cattle and drovers for a few days before completing the journey to her new property. The journey from Broome had taken five months of very hard work and riding. She established her homestead on the banks of Ethel creek and named her station Glen Carrick Downs, after the region where she was born in Ireland. Today that station is still in production, however the new owners have changed the name to Ethel Creek.

Glen Carrick station is about 170 kilometres north-east from the town of Mt Newman that is the site of one of the largest iron ore mines in the world. From Glen Carrick the Ophthalmia ranges can be seen in the distance.

Word spread far and wide in the Aboriginal world about Daisy providing food in the form of bully beef, flour, tea and sugar in return for help in building the cattle station. Many Aboriginal families arrived to set up their humpies a short distance from the homestead. Over a number of years Daisy Bates provided regular food, medical care and advice to the Aboriginal families who lived on the Glen Carrick property.

From the beginning of this arrangement Daisy learnt to speak their language, understand their customs and found herself easily communicating with them. Several years later some of the Aboriginal men had become experienced enough to operate the cattle and other tasks on the station alone, so Daisy took a journey with her horse and wagonette to Perth – another 1600 kilometres through bush to the south.

Through her acquaintance with Father Martelli she became friendly with the Bishop of Perth, and through him associated with people in power in Government.

In 1910 the Colonial secretary proposed she accompany an international expedition through a very remote part of Western Australia. This expedition was to be led by Professor Radcliff Brown, an anthropologist from Cambridge University in England. It included several other scientists, including Grant Watson, a government botanist and a photographer. On this expedition Daisy Bates was given permission to conduct an inquiry into the health and working conditions of natives employed by sheep and cattle stations and the rapidly developing problem of half-castes being born around the mining centres.

The first camp was established near Sandstone, a small mining centre north-west of Kalgoorlie. A large number of Aborigines soon gathered near the camp when word spread that food, tea, sugar and tobacco were being given to the natives. Some Aborigines recognised Daisy because they had met her on her journey south. Because of her knowledge of the native language she was very helpful to Professor Brown and the other scientists. They held council with many tribal groups from a wide area in the north-west during their 15-month-long expedition. They returned to Perth after gaining much knowledge.

A few months after they returned from their expedition Daisy became ill and decided to have a holiday in Sydney, once again sailing on a windjammer to cross the very rough sea of the Great Australian Bight. She spent six months visiting and staying with old friends in Tasmania and Sydney. There is no evidence to suggest that she met her ex-husband John Bates on this visit.

Returning to Perth, she was saddened to learn that a tribal man from the Sandstone area had been arrested for murder and that another five men from the same area had also been arrested. From her previous visits to the Sandstone area she knew this man and doubted his guilt.

She requested an opportunity to visit these men in jail and permission was granted. On arrival at the jail she immediately recognised five of the men who were not from the Sandstone area. They were from the region of Daisy's Glen Carrick cattle station. They had come south to see Daisy Bates after they had heard she had been in the Sandstone area.

After interviewing the men and hearing their stories she sought permission to represent them in court. Permission was again granted.

During the trial Daisy explained to the judge that the first man from Sandstone charged with murder had only carried out his duties to his elders. It was a case where a tribal man had committed a very serious crime breaking the laws of marriage. This crime was punishable by death.

"The man you have arrested and charged with murder is in the same position as the white man executioner who will be ordered to put to death this man you have on trial." The trial judge listened intently to the defence of this Aboriginal prisoner by the brilliant Daisy Bates.

He remarked to her, "You are so knowledgeable about the affairs of our native people. I find the prisoner not guilty." On record, that was the first time an arrested Aboriginal had not been taken to the gallows to die by the hangman's noose.

In representing the five other men, Daisy Bates was able to prove they did not even belong to that area. They were only visitors passing through on their search for her as they were from her station in the north.

"I have interviewed the policemen who arrested the prisoners and I was told they were in the area when we searched for the murderer. One black nigger is the same as any other black nigger."

Because of the brilliant defence of the prisoners by Daisy the judge released the prisoners to return to their families at Ethel Creek Station.

About this time Daisy decided to sell her cattle station because she was very much involved in other projects assisting in health and justice administrated by the Government. She also considered that the money from the sale of the cattle station could be put to better use for the benefit of the native people.

The next emergency was an outbreak of measles and whooping cough in the Greenbushes and Katanning region of the south-west. Daisy once more loaded her wagonette with camping gear and food and travelled to Greenbushes to set up a medical centre. To stop the epidemic she segregated the children with the disease, then nursed the patients back to good health. Thousands of children were saved who without her actions would have died.

Another very serious epidemic causing the Government health authorities great concern, was the outbreak of leprosy and tuberculosis in the Pilbara. In this area north-west of Carnarvon to the Ophthalmia ranges, Daisy's cattle station country, thousands of native people were dying without any medical assistance. Finally, with encouragement from Daisy the Government set up two makeshift medical centres on two deserted islands.

The Government plans were to segregate all the native people who were infected with either of the diseases, then round them up and take them from their tribal land to one of the islands in Shark Bay. The women were sent to Dorre Island and the men to Bernier Island. The authorities gave no thought to the fact that these people were all from different tribes and different tribal country. In some cases they were hostile enemies of one another. It is not generally known that of the hundreds of tribes all over Australia, most were continually at war with each other. Very often one tribe would not even be able to speak the same dialect of other tribes. This ignorance by the Government resulted in the death of people not only from the diseases, but also from fighting when they were all lumped together.

To find the natives with the diseases, Government troopers would ride their horses into the tribal lands, inspected any they found and if contaminated then chain the unfortunate people by the neck, tie them all together and make them walk behind the trooper's horses. Sometimes they were made to walk for hundreds of kilometres to Carnarvon where they would be taken by canoe to the islands in the bay – 30 kilometres from shore.

Once on the islands there were very primitive facilities and almost no medical treatment available. Consequently, hundreds of people died each week. Many died from the conditions and fear of being away from their tribal land and their loved ones. Once again, Daisy set out from Perth to travel along the bush tracks to Carnarvon to see for herself the conditions provided by the Government.

On arrival on the islands of Dorre and Bernier she was shocked, appalled and devastated to find desperately sick people lying around. Some with no shade or shelter and particularly no medical treatment. Dead bodies could be found all over the islands.

Taking it upon herself to do something, she started writing letters to the various Government officials she knew. However she seldom got a reply, let alone any help. She found herself not only devastated, but also incredibly helpless. In desperation, she decided that the first thing she could do was provide some medical assistance with her own money. She also thought she must try to lift their spirits, give them some hope of recovery and return them to their homeland.

Daisy quickly she set out with her horse and wagonette to travel hundreds of kilometres into the different tribal lands of many of the patients she had met on the islands. Meeting these families of the sick she gathered many messages to be delivered to the patients. At the same time she encouraged many tribal leaders to form a message service by having fit strong young men travel from their areas to Carnarvon.

On arrival at Carnarvon, Daisy organised local Aborigines to transport these messenger men in canoes to deliver the individual family message. They would sit down in a shaded area with each patient and talk to them about their loved ones. The messengers would then return by canoe and start running, in some cases hundreds of kilometres back to their tribal lands to deliver their responses.

You may have heard or read that the native people

sometimes carry message sticks on some journeys, implying that the message is cut into the message stick. This is incorrect information. In fact the stick has cuts in it only to remind the messenger how many messages he has memorised.

Almost immediately Daisy could see a great improvement in many of the patients' attitude. They now had the determination to live and beat their disease in order to be able to return to their families.

Daisy often sat for hours talking to the ill and at times some of these poor souls died in her arms.

On one such occasion she was nursing a very ill old man who was weak and dying. He explained to her that he was frightened because as he was not in his tribal land his spirit would be lost forever. The old man looked up into Daisy's eyes and said, "Kabbarli, where am I going?"

Daisy replied, "You are going where my father is."

The old man said, "Kabbarli, with your father I will be safe." He then died peacefully in her arms. The word *Kabbarli* in Aboriginal mythology means *Dreamtime Grandmother*. Daisy Bates was known throughout the land as Kabbarli.

Daisy Bates' work and assistance to these unfortunate people of the north-west saved lives and made it possible for many to return to their families.

For her incredible devotion to humanity, Queen

Victoria awarded Daisy Bates the honour of C.B.E – Commander of the British Empire.

On completion of her work at Dorre and Bernier Islands, Daisy returned to Perth, where she became involved in some intensive study of the races and cultures for the government of Western Australia.

Several years later she was once again loading her wagonette and harnessing her horse and travelling away from civilisation, this time to regions around Albany to gather information on the health of the local Aboriginal people in those areas. After spending some time on research in the Esperance region she moved on to Eucla, where she made her permanent camp for more than 10 years. Eucla is on the coast of the western side of the Nullarbor Plain.

Daisy Bates was now the official protector of Aboriginal people.

At Eucla camp she was able to confirm some of the history of Australia that had occurred more than 65 years before. During her research studies and enquiries she learnt the fate of explorer John Eyre's second-in-command, Captain Baxter.

It was around the time when John Eyre was attempting to make the first crossing of Australia. One day Eyre left Baxter and two native guides in camp whilst he and another native guide went off in search of water. In his absence the two natives attacked Captain Baxter and killed him with a blow to the head. They then made off with the rations, two shotguns and most of the water. Daisy learnt that the Aborigines, who had been watching from bushes high up on the cliffs, then ambushed and killed the murderers.

John Eyre returned to camp and was shocked and saddened at the scene before him. His good friend and deputy Captain Baxter lay face down, dead, with gaping wounds to his head.

The next day John Eyre and his one trusted guide Wylie, left camp after covering Baxter's body with a canvas sheet. It was not possible to dig a grave in the hard limestone country.

John Eyre and Wylie finally arrived at the small settlement of Albany and returned to Adelaide on a sailing ship.

In 1914, Daisy was invited by the Commonwealth Government to deliver a paper on Australian Aboriginal lives and customs at an international convention in Adelaide. The journey of travelling 1300 kilometres across the Nullarbor Plain presented little problem for such an adventurous woman. She swapped her horses for a camel and also bought another camel from an Aboriginal man (there are thousands of wild camels in outback Australia originally imported for the Burke and

Wills expedition.)

One camel pulled the wagonette and the second camel, driven by an old Aboriginal and his wife, pulled a cart loaded with food and water drums for crossing the dry desert Nullarbor Plain.

Travelling 32 kilometres a day, this unusual group arrived in Port Augusta about six weeks later. At Port Augusta Daisy made arrangements for her Aboriginal friends, two camels, and wagonette to be accommodated until her return. She then continued her journey from Port Augusta to Adelaide by train.

After the convention, several weeks later, Daisy caught the train back to Port Augusta only to find that her two Aboriginal friends, husband and wife, had become homesick, taken their camels, and returned without the wagonette and cart to their home in Eucla.

Spending a few days in Port Augusta, Daisy watched with interest as hundreds of men were being engaged by the railways to work building the train line from Port Augusta to Kalgoorlie, which would connect with the Western Australia line to Perth. Equipment and thousands of sleepers and rail lines were being stored in the yards ready for transport to the railhead for the line across the Nullarbor. Along the route many small villages were built to accommodate the workmen's families. These small villages were starting to attract many Aboriginal groups, some from great distances away, who set up camp nearby in the bush.

Daisy made up her mind to establish her new camp in one of these villages, where she could keep an eye on the health and well-being of many Aboriginal people.

After studying the route of the railway line, and talking to some Aborigines from this side of the Nullarbor, she selected Ooldea waterhole as her new home for the next 25 years. She had been told that Ooldea waterhole was a place all travelling Aborigines passed through because it was a crossroad on the great trading route.

Throughout Australia, great trading routes have existed for thousands of years. Along these trading routes native people had traded goods and chattels and, in some cases, women from afar. Ochre would be carried from places like the Flinders Ranges in South Australia to the limestone country of the Nullarbor Plain. The Nullarbor Plain Aboriginal people would carry bags of seashells and shark teeth for decorations for the Central Australian natives. On their return they would bring back flint stones from the McDonnell Ranges to be made into flint knives and spearheads. The famous Warramunga tribe of the Tennant Creek area were probably the greatest traders in Australia because they lived in an area with huge supplies of lancewood, which is wonderful for spears and as straight as a gun barrel. Their products of spears, woomeras and boomerangs were always in great demand. So the trade routes crossed Australia from north to south, and east to west, for thousands of years. This made Daisy realise that she could meet native people easily by using the trading routes, and in turn help people she may never have had the fortune of meeting.

By the time she set up her camp at Ooldea waterhole, Kabbarli was well known to the Aboriginal people of that country. They had all heard about her, through word of mouth, from travellers passing that way over many years.

With the help of the local natives she set up her camp in the bush about half a kilometre from the village. The Aboriginal men built a shade house with a bush-made table and canvas deck chair alongside her tent. They also built a brush fence around her camping area. Often Daisy would spend hours in her shade house writing her critical letters to politicians, magazines and newspapers or making notes on her environment.

Thousands of train travellers on the transcontinental train would remember stopping at the small siding of Ooldea and seeing a little old lady immaculately dressed in Victorian period clothes, a long skirt, spotless white blouse, with a hat decorated with fruit and flowers.

In semi high-heeled shoes she would be pushing her wheelbarrow of food supplies down a little track from the train station to her home – a tent in the bush. The supplies she collected from the guards' van. The train travellers of that time would also remember the many Aborigines, hawking their boomerangs and other souvenirs.

The Transcontinental line attracted Aborigines to the area from hundreds of kilometres away. Many Aboriginal families, from places such as Ayers Rock (Uluru) and Hermannsburg, moved south to the train line. Many generations of their families were born along the Trans line. Most travelled back to their original tribal land in the early 1960s when the trains started operating with diesel engines and no longer stopped at these little sidings.

One notable visitor at Ooldea to meet Daisy in 1920 was his Royal Highness the Duke of Gloucester. On his Transcontinental crossing to Perth he asked especially that his itinerary include a meeting with Daisy at the station at Ooldea. The world press displayed a photo of her meeting the Duke.

Daisy Bates died in Adelaide in 1951 at the age of 91, She is buried in the Enfield cemetery at North Adelaide.

There are hundreds of stories she told the world of her strange life with the Aborigines. Many books, magazines and newspaper articles have told some of them.

There will never be another Daisy Bates.

She was so familiar with the lives and customs of the Aboriginal people and to gain this knowledge she lived in the bush with them for more than sixty years. Modern day anthropologists jealously negate much of her writing. They fail to realise that many of her stories are based on what the Aborigines believed, such as the following.

Around 1915, not long after she first came to live at Ooldea waterhole, some old Aborigines told her that there was to be a huge corroboree near Eucla on the western side of the Nullarbor Plain. Many white people think that a corroboree means a dance where it actually means a gathering of people. Just as we in the white world enjoy a gathering of friends, we may talk for a while and maybe dance a little. So it is in their world. There are little family corroborees that may be held every week. Then there are tribal corroborees, and district tribal corroborees that may be held once a year. About every 25 or 30 years they hold a huge corroboree that involves people from all over Australia. At the conclusion of each meeting the date and the meeting place is agreed on for the next year. The date is tabulated by the elders of each tribe, marking on sticks the number of moons till the next meeting. The elders of each tribe pass down this information. In some cases the tribal elders travelling to distant meetings may be walking for several months to get to the meeting place.

The meetings are normally to discuss tribal borders or laws and changes to such. Nearly every tribe has slightly different rules or laws to one another. One of the only beliefs that they all agree to is the law of the Rainbow Serpent who was the maker of all things on the planet.

Daisy, on hearing the news of the huge corroboree, made plans to attend. By now her camels were gone and her old wagonette and cart had fallen to pieces. She therefore planned to walk across the 1300 kilometres of the Nullarbor Plain in the company of the Ooldea tribal elders.

So the journey began. The very hot summer had passed and the weather was quite mild as they set out. It would be as strange a scene as it is possible to see. Just imagine Daisy Bates striding out in the front of this procession dressed in her neat Victorian era dress down to her ankles, spotless white blouse, and a hat with imitation fruit and flowers arranged around the crown, with a fly veil. She would be holding a large umbrella to provide shade from the hot sun. In her other hand she would be carrying her satchel with her precious writing pads and notebooks. Following behind her a hundred completely naked tribesmen carrying spears, woomeras, and boomerangs, along with Daisy's tent and tent poles, cooking equipment, pots and pans, and even one naked warrior carrying her suitcase. Daisy had no trouble communicating with her companions as she spoke well over one hundred dialects. Five weeks later the Ooldea group arrived at the meeting place near Eucla.

The tribesmen erected her tent and built a shade house with bush-table and seat for Daisy to sit and write her notes of the events to follow.

Her camp was approximately 700 metres from the Corroboree site. In the Corroboree area there were more than one thousand tribal elders present.

Daisy sat in her shade house and all day tribal elders came to visit her. She was delighted to meet old friends from places such as Sandstone, Greenbushes and the Flinders Ranges, and she was especially pleased to greet an old friend who as a young man she had nursed on Bernier Island.

Sadly a friend from Broome brought news that Father Martelli at the ripe old age of 96, had passed away at the Beagle Bay mission a few years before.

When all visitors had arrived the Corroboree got underway. To begin proceedings, everyone sat down to get to know each other before beginning any serious talks.

Later, to the haunting sound of a dozen didgeridoos, and the beating of time with clap-sticks and boomerangs, the dancing begins. Around a large fire a circle of several hundred people dancing vigorously and thumping the ground with their feet, causes the dust to fly. Daisy told of the ground shaking beneath her feet from 700 metres away, as the dancers continued throughout the night. The singers joined in too.

Some of these dancers went on for up to 30 hours without stopping. Often dancers fell down in the dust completely exhausted and the dance went on with a hundred feet dancing around them on the ground. When they recovered they got up and rejoined in the dancing once again.

Daisy, as was her usual custom, rose at the piccaninny dawn and lit her campfire to boil water for her first cup of tea for the day. Whilst waiting for the water to boil she did her daily washing. Even in the primitive conditions that she lived in, she was always spotlessly dressed. After completing her washing chores she sat down to enjoy her drink.

Looking toward the corroboree gathering, and listening to the didgeridoo music and the chanting of the hundreds of singers, she noticed two Aboriginal men coming towards her camp. As they came closer she recognised the men as her friends from Ooldea. Suddenly she became worried as she watched the way the men walked. They had hunched shoulders, arms hanging down their sides, with feet dragging in the dirt, and head bowed. This is generally a sign of distress or sadness. The men approached Daisy and said, "Kabbarli, we bring you very much sad news."

"Well, men, what is the sad news you bring me?" asked Daisy.

"Kabbarli," one of the men answered, "Nukarla died last night."

Daisy was badly shocked and saddened. Nukarla was one of the great tribal leaders of the Ooldea people, and her great friend and confidant of the tribe. She had known his father, his children, and grand children. After delivering their sad message the men turned to walk back towards the Corroboree when Daisy called out.

"Just a minute, men. Come back here, I want you to explain something to me."

The men returned to her side.

Daisy Bates at Ooldea Camp by Margot Vaughan

"This morning," Daisy said, "as I hung my washing over there under that dry mulga tree, my blouse suddenly became soaking wet from water pouring from a branch of that tree. As you can see now my blouse is dripping wet. I looked up into the clear blue sky and saw that it could not be rain. What is the meaning of this?" she asked. One of the men replied. "Kabbarli, that is easy to explain. That tree you hung your washing under is a Nala tree (wild currant tree). That tree is Nukarla's totem. The edible bark tree is Nukarla. In this dry country water is the most precious thing to give. He is saying to you thank you, Kabbarli, for being so good, kind and helpful to my family and for all you have done for my tribe at Ooldea, and all Aboriginal people. Also he says Bor Bor. Good bye."

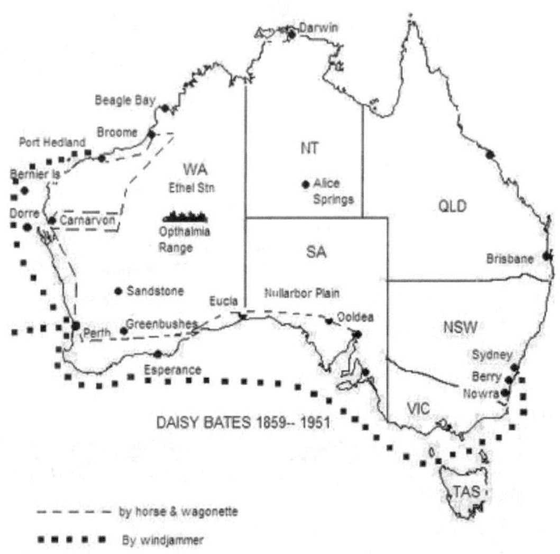

# *Sister Ruth, Bush Nurse*

Around the campfires of the outback many stories are told of heroic deeds performed by our pioneers – both men and women.

Few stories of heroics can exceed those of the brave and dedicated efforts of Mrs Ruth Heathcock, wife of mounted constable Ted Heathcock, stationed at the remote outpost of Borroloola in the Northern Territory.

Situated 50 kilometres inland from the western shores of the Gulf of Carpentaria was the base for both the mounted policeman and his wife, Government Bush Nurse Sister Ruth.

It was February 1941, the middle of the tropical rainy season. It had so far been a very big wet-season with much of the countryside flooded. Late one afternoon Sister Ruth could hear the heavy rain falling on the corrugated iron roof of her home. She listened to the loud claps of thunder and saw the flashes of lightning. She thought of her husband somewhere in the outback, over 160 kilometres away, on horseback patrol. She hoped he was safe in a cave or rock shelter, out of this terrible storm.

Suddenly there was a loud knocking on her front door. Alarmed she rushed to it and upon opening saw two completely exhausted Aboriginal men lying on her doorstep. Looking up at Sister Ruth, one of the men, with urgency in his voice, called out, "Sister Ruth, Sister Ruth, come quick! Horace Foster has shot his legs with double barrel shot gun."

Sister Ruth ushered the two men into the house and they lay on the carpet floor. She covered them with blankets and dried them with towels as they relayed their story to her. Sister Ruth fed them with hot soup and beef stew.

Horace Foster was well known to her, and she thought of the long trip these two men must have made over flooded rivers on their mercy mission. Horace Foster lived on Manangoora Cattle station, out on the banks of the Wearyan River, about 80 kilometres from Borroloola, near the coast of the Gulf of Carpentaria. He had been out on the river in his dinghy, fishing and shooting ducks. As he stepped ashore from his dinghy the gun he was carrying accidentally discharged, blasting both his legs.

The only people there at the time were the two station Aboriginal stockmen. After carrying Foster up to the top of the riverbank they decided not to carry him all the way to his house 800 metres away because of his terrible injuries.

Instead they made a bed of leaves and built a brush shade over him. After leaving him with a billycan of water they set off on their cross-country run over the flooded country for 80 kilometres to Borroloola.

Crocodiles inhabited many of the rivers they crossed and they often had to jump over deadly snakes that lay on the higher ground of the bush tracks. All night the men ran, soaking wet from the tropical rain and swimming the flooded rivers on and on until they arrived at Sister Ruth's house. As the two men sat resting in front of the open fire Sister Ruth offered them dry clothes. She knew she could do nothing until the flying doctor radio came on service the next morning.

At 7am sharp, Sister Ruth contacted the flying doctor in far away Cloncurry, Queensland, a distance of over 800 kilometres.

When the flying doctor heard her story of Horace Foster's predicament, he said he would immediately take off in his light aircraft. During the next five hours the light plane struggled against cyclonic gale-force winds and blinding rainstorms to finally arrive overhead at the Manangoora homestead.

However the flying doctor immediately could see that the salt flat, which he usually landed on, was flooded with water. He radioed Sister Ruth that he was unable to land . The two Aboriginal messenger men had recovered after a good night's sleep in beds Sister Ruth had provided. Sister Ruth gave them the news that the flying doctor was unable to go to the assistance of Horace Foster. With distress in their voice they offered another alternative to Sister Ruth. They would gather three of their friends who lived in Borroloola and take her in a dugout wooden canoe to Manangoora station to bring help to the injured man.

The dangers were quite apparent to Sister Ruth. Travelling down the mighty McArthur River in a flooding raging torrent would be extremely dangerous. However, Sister Ruth refused to accept defeat. She was determined to go to the injured man's assistance, even if it meant losing her own life. Shortly after the two Aborigines had made their brave offer, the five men and Sister Ruth were busy loading the frail dugout canoe with a small supply of food and water. She carried her precious little box of medical supplies in a backpack.

When the six brave people got into the canoe there were only a few inches of freeboard above the waterline. They had to paddle 72 kilometres to the mouth of the McArthur River to reach the open sea, then travel another 19 kilometres along the coast, beyond the mangrove swamps to the mouth of the Wearyan River. From there it was another 16 kilometres to Manangoora station, where the injured man lay on the riverbank.

All set to begin the life-and-death struggle down the flooded river, one man stood with one foot in the canoe and the other foot on the muddy riverbank.

"We go now," the man called as he pushed off from the bank. Soon they were being buffeted in huge whirlpools and currents, with many large trees floating in the raging river and at times crashing into the frail canoe.

Sister Ruth on McArthur River by Margot Vaughan.

On several occasions, large man-eating crocodiles, which manoeuvred frighteningly around the small craft, were snapping at the paddles as the men fought furiously against the forces of nature.

After three hours of battling down the McArthur River the open ocean appeared in view. Mounting anguish was in the minds of the canoe's occupants as the small craft left the river. The men turned the craft head on into the rough sea, which made Sister Ruth extremely anxious. She felt very much responsible for the five brave men she had placed in this dangerous position. The water splashed over the gunwales and Sister Ruth was kept very busy as she continued bailing the water from the bottom of the canoe. Still there was more terror to come. Large sea snakes could be seen swimming beneath the canoe and occasionally a large tiger shark. Now they were in a critical part of their risky adventure as they travelled along the coastline beyond the dangerous mangrove swamps. Tragedy to all in the canoe would result if it floundered and drifted into those dangerous mangrove swamps.

The journey along the 19 kilometres of coastline was probably the most dangerous. The hot sun was now starting to disappear into the hills to the west. In one way this was a blessing as it was terribly hot in the open canoe, however, as darkness set in, Sister Ruth began to worry that the men would not be able to find the entrance to the Wearyan River. The tropical storm of rain, thunder and lightning added to the discomfort of the occupants of the canoe. The Aboriginals encouraged Sister Ruth with the suggestion that they were all safe as they were water people. They and their ancestors had battled against these elements of nature for thousands of years. Near midnight, the canoe men steered the frail craft without error up the centre of the Wearyan River. Now there were only 16 kilometres to travel to the homestead and the critically injured man.

This river was also in flood, with as many hazards as had been experienced in the McArthur River. The men battled all night against the floodwaters. As the sun rose in the morning the brave little group came in view of the homestead and soon approached the wounded man, lying still under the shade cover the men had built to protect him.

Jumping ashore Sister Ruth was shocked at the condition of Horace Foster. Before attending to his terribly shattered and mutilated legs, she recognised the evidence of fatal tetanus showing in Foster's twitching face. The muscle spasms were drawing back his lips. She firstly administered anti-tetanus serum. Then she inserted a tube into his mouth and fed him fluids. Then came the sickening task of cleaning the putrid congealed blood clots and rotting flesh hanging from his legs. Ants and blowflies had already found and infiltrated his wounds.

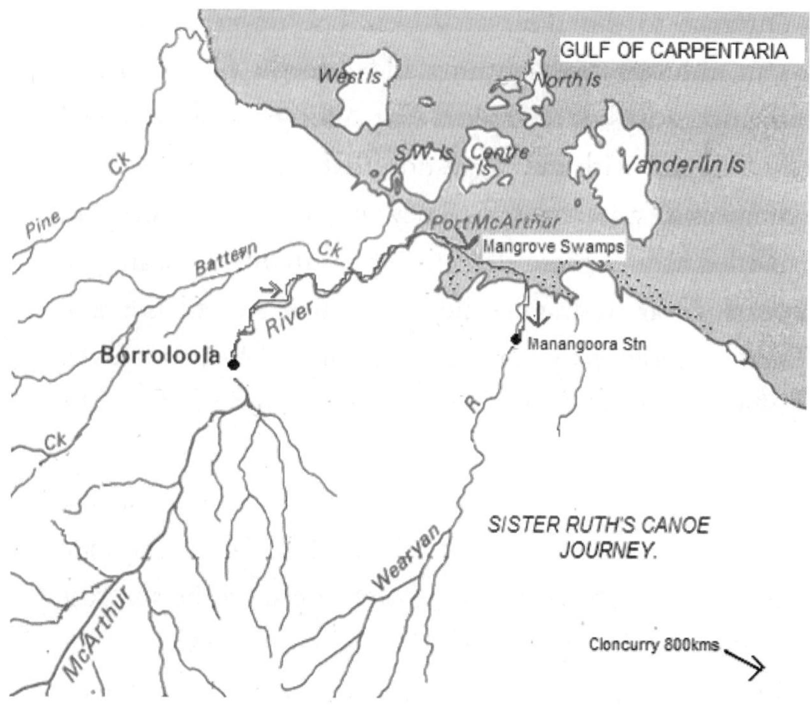


The sickly stench of gangrene hung over all. Sister Ruth worked all day on the injuries and kept feeding fluids along with painkillers to try and relieve the man's pain.

Foster's neighbours, Tom Kieran and Stuart McIntyre rode in after hearing of the tragedy on the Aborigine's message service. They carried the desperately ill man on a stretcher made of a bullock's hide to his homestead. The two men then turned their attention to making another airstrip on higher ground. Gathering a number of Aboriginal station stockmen, who had also ridden in, they started clearing the scrub and stones for the new airstrip.

Stuart decided to make a dash on horseback to Borroloola, 80 kilometres away over flooded country, in order to get a radio message over to the flying doctor to let him know that the new landing ground would soon be available.

Not long after the horseman had departed, the blast of a horn could be heard on the river. Aaround the river bend came the small trading steamer Noosa, that usually called at the station about once a month to bring supplies. Captain John Rusher, a long time friend of Foster, was devastated on learning the news. He immediately turned his ship around and raced downstream. He knew he could be back in Borroloola long before Stuart McIntyre arrived on horseback. On arrival at Borroloola, Captain Rusher sent a radio message to the flying doctor in Cloncurry, that a new airstrip had been cleared and it would now be safe to land at Manangoora Station. The flying doctor on hearing this news, once again took off on his flight of mercy. The weather had cleared and the flying conditions were much improved.

Back at Manangoora station, Sister Ruth still battled in her attempt to keep her patient alive. She was much relieved when she heard the roar of the flying doctor's plane landing.

Looking out the window as she held Horace Foster in her arms, she saw the doctor jump down from his plane and run to a saddled horse. Now he was galloping toward the homestead. At that moment Sister Ruth felt Horace Foster shiver and shake. He died in her arms, the flying doctor just seconds too late. However, he probably could not have saved the severely injured Foster.

At this point we think of the incredible sacrifices and bravery of those Aboriginal men, especially the two who first brought the bad news to Sister Ruth in Borroloola, and the immediate and dangerous action as taken on that occasion by Sister Ruth.

Forty-seven years later, in 1988, Sister Ruth Heathcock died in Darwin aged 100 years. Sister Ruth will always be remembered for the dedication and sacrifices she made during a lifetime of nursing service in the Australian outback.

# *It's a Long Dusty Road*

A city travelling salesman was transferred to operate in the Queensland outback. Out on the track his car broke down. He could see in the distance, at the end of the long dusty road, a farmhouse. He walked and he walked to the lonely farmhouse. As he approached, all the sheep-dogs were barking.

A farmer met him at the door. The travelling salesman explained that his car had broken down and he would have to radio for a part to be sent from the city. He then asked the farmer if he could give him accommodation for a few days. The farmer called his wife and said, "This gentleman's car has broken down and he has asked if we could put him up for a few days."

"Well, yes," replied the farmer's wife. "However we are a bit short on meat. We'll have to kill one of those young boars." So they killed a pig and butchered it. Over the next few days they almost lived off that pig.

Roast pork for dinner, pork chops for breakfast. The farmer's wife even made some brawn from the pig's head. On the last morning of the travellers stay they had bacon and eggs for breakfast. The visitor told the woman that the bacon was a bit salty and asked if he could please have a drink of water?

The farmer's wife brought him a glass of water. He took a mouthful of the water and spat it out. "What did you put in that water?"

"I put nothing in the water. It's bore water."

"Heck," said the visitor, "you don't waste much of that pig, do you?"

# *Northern Territory Cattle Station*

Some cattle stations in the Northern Territory are the largest in the world. For instance, Victoria River Downs is 10,000 square kilometres. The number of cattle on that run would be sround eighty thousand head. Many parts of the property are rarely visited. Helicopters, with a little help from horsemen, do the mustering.

I once asked a cattle station owner, "How many cattle do you run on this property?"

Somewhat baffled, he replied, "Oh um ah, maybe twenty, ah thirty, or forty thousand head."

# *Harry Redford, Outback Gambler*

In 1870, the most remote cattle station in South Australia was Blanchewater Station, established by John Baker in 1857.

Situated on the MacDonnell watercourse, which flows into Lake Blanche, an outstation, some 30 kilometres to the east, was established on a large waterhole at Mt Hopeless Creek. To the south lie the rugged Northern Flinders Ranges.

The month of June is winter mustering time.

The station stockmen were busy at work. The cattle were being mustered on the vast plains and along the shores of Lake Callabonna.

The fats are selected for sale and cut from the mob.

The yearlings are earmarked and branded and the young bulls castrated.

It had been a very hot and dusty day in the saddle. The men had been riding hard since sun rise. They were tired and thankful the long day was coming to an end. Each rider made his way over to a large cluster of trees by the side of a dry creek. In the shade of the large gum trees were the cook's wagon and campfire, and the camp cook was preparing the evening meal.

As each rider rode into camp and dismounted he would throw the reins over the horse's head and latch it to a small tree. Taking the saddle off and placing it upright leaning against a tree, he would wipe the sweat from the horses back with the saddle cloth, then arrange the cloth over a bush to dry and air during the night. Depending on the temperament of his horse, a rider would place hobbles on its front legs. After taking the bridle off, he would give his horse a pat on the rump and send it off to graze along the bank of the creek for the night. The men then gathered around the large campfire discussing the day's events. Some rolled cigarettes whilst they waited for the cook to ring his bell and call, "Come and get it."

One of the men in the group pointed to the north where the big red sun was setting over the Cobbler desert.

"What is causing that big cloud of dust out yonder

when there is very little wind?"

All the men studied this strange scene for several seconds when one remarked, "Maybe it's a large mob of emus."

"I've never seen a mob of emus make that much dust," another remarked. "More like a mob of cattle."

"Cattle?" they called in unison. "No cattle out that way. Nobody has been out in that desert since Burke and Wills perished at Cooper Creek ten years ago."

Suddenly a voice shouted, "It's cattle! Of that I am sure."

Another man spoke up, "My goodness, I think you are right. I can see horsemen moving in the dust behind them."

The evening meal was forgotten as the men watched the amazing scene developing before their eyes. Shortly after, four drovers stopped the cattle on the other side of the creek. They had spotted the campfire and the group of men watching. With a wave of the hand the drovers dismounted and walked across the dry creek to the camp. After introducing themselves to the stockmen they explained to the intrigued group that they had travelled all the way from Queensland to seek a better price for their animals. The prices in Brisbane and northern New South Wales at that time were very low. They thought that they would get a better price in Adelaide.

The head stockman, Alan Walke, estimated the

number of cattle was about 800 or a 1000 head. He advised the drovers that cattle prices recently in Adelaide had been good as a result of good rains in the autumn. He noticed that amongst the mob of cattle was a big white bull that he judged to be well-bred. Walke told the drovers that he would immediately ride back to the homestead to report to the station manager, Mr Jim Mules, of the arrival of the group. The leader of the drovers then asked Walke to ask his boss if he would sell them two bags of flour, some tea, sugar and tinned butter as their supplies were getting low. On arrival at the homestead, Walke gave his boss the news and suggested that amongst the drover's mob of cattle was a well-bred English bull that he may be interested in buying. Jim Mules ordered Walke to load the requested supplies from the storeroom onto the two-in-hand wagonette and harness the horses early in the morning. He would depart at sun rise to go to the outstation.

After meeting the drovers, Mr Mules asked if they would sell him the white bull and several hundred of the cattle.

"Sure," replied the leader of the drovers. They quickly agreed on a price that included the supplies from the storeroom. Several of the stockmen saddled their horses and cut the bull and several hundred of the cattle from the mob and drove them back towards the Blanchewater homestead paddock. As the drovers were making ready to continue their journey, a stockmen with a stick in hand drew a mud map on the ground as to the best route for the drovers to take.

They were advised to travel down the eastern side of the ranges where they would find plenty of watering holes.

"When you arrive near the end of these ranges you will find a large pound. The pound has only one small entrance. You can drive your cattle into this pound and close off the entrance. Your cattle can be rested on the good sweet grass in the pound before you continue on to Adelaide with your cattle in good condition."

*This pound today is known as Wilpena Pound. For many years the Rasheed family owners of Wilpena Station preserved the fence posts built by Harry Redford until they were destroyed by fire in 1958.*

The drovers eventually arrived with their cattle in Adelaide. The cattle brought top price at the sales at Gepps Cross. After the leader of the drovers received the cash for the cattle it was evenly divided between the four men and each man went his separate way.

Harry Redford was born at Mudgee and raised at Brooklyn by the Hawkesbury River in New South Wales. At 14 years of age he was a big strong lad. He left home and went to the goldfields at Hill End and Bathurst. Hard work was not one of his favourite pastimes. Instead he worked in gambling houses and became a card shark. And before long became an expert poker player and a cheat.

Money came easily to Harry Redford. He was always extremely well-dressed in the latest fashions and rode a thoroughbred horse. It was always well-groomed with a smartly polished bridle and saddle. He turned heads wherever he rode.

Harry Redford invented the game of bush two-up. The format of bush two-up is similar to the old Australian game of two-up played with pennies. However, in camp, drovers don't carry pennies.

Harry Redford's bush two-up was played with a stockman's lanyard, not coins. Both players contribute to a game purse, say, 10 shillings each to start. Harry Redford was a very good talker. The following is how his repertoire would go:

"OK, I will put the lanyard down as a figure eight. Now when you place your finger in one of the loops, one loop will hold your finger and the other one won't. It is like heads or tails. So who is going to play first? OK, Charlie, you're gonna give it a go. Best of luck. I'll give you a few tries to get you familiar with the game. I lay the lanyard down in a figure eight like so. Now, Charlie, you put your finger in one of the loops. Now I pull the rope and if you have chosen the right end that will hold your finger, you win. If the rope pulls clear I win.

OK. Now, Charlie, put your finger in the loop that will hold. Of course, I don't lay the rope down the same end each time I change it from one end to the other."

After a few practise runs he says. "You seem to have picked up how to play quicker than most. Now here we go for keeps. The purse is 10 shillings each. I lay the lanyard down now put your finger in the one that will hold your finger, Charlie. There that's great, you win 20 shillings.

"We set up the purse again, Charlie. You say to double the bet this time. OK. The purse is 40 shillings each. Put your finger in the one that will hold your finger. Not the one that doesn't. Great, Charlie, I can see you're gonna send me broke. You win 80 shillings. See how easy it is. Charlie, here we go again. This time it's for 160 shillings. You say you have not got that much money to

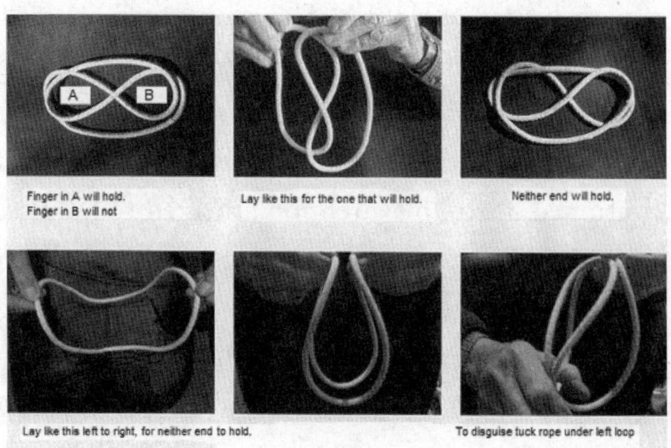


Finger in A will hold.
Finger in B will not

Lay like this for the one that will hold.

Neither end will hold.

Lay like this left to right, for neither end to hold.

To disguise tuck rope under left loop

contribute to the purse. I'll tell you what you can do. Put up what you have already won plus your horse. I'll put my thoroughbred horse in also. You agree? Right, here we go. Oh, bad luck, Charlie. You lose. Which one was your horse Charlie? OK Bill, you can have a go now."

Of course it's the old thimble and the pea trick in a different form. It is possible to lay the rope down so neither end will hold your finger.

After several years around the gambling houses of Bathurst and Hill End his reputation as a poker player and gambler indicated to him it was time to move on. The latest gold rush was in the far off Northern Territory. Harry Redford set off on the long ride along the Castlereagh Track. Hundreds of men were making that journey, some in wagons, spring carts, buggies, even pushbikes. Others walked humping their swags. All the travellers along the Castlereagh Track at that time must have envied their fellow traveller riding his thoroughbred horse with his fancy clothes. They continued along the Castlereagh Track, following the Warrego River through Charleville. There is no evidence to show that Redford visited his second eldest brother who worked near Judah. He continued north, his attention attracted to hundreds of prime conditioned cattle grazing on Mitchell and Flinders grass as high as an elephant's eye, on the rolling hills of the channel country. The station he was passing through was Bowen Downs. As he rode that afternoon he devised a plan he believed could work in his favour. Tomorrow morning he would call into the homestead seeking employment.

In company with William Cornish and William Landsborough, Nat Buchanan had established the first cattle station in outback Queensland. They called their station Bowen Downs. Landsborough and D'Arcy Uhr had discovered these rolling plains in 1862 on their return from searching for Burke and Wills in the Gulf area.

The station ran approximately 60,000 head of well-bred cattle on their 3000 square kilometres of country. The station homestead was built in typical Queensland-style, up on stilts, to escape the floodwaters of Cornish Creek during the tropical rainy season.

As the sun came up in the early morn, Nat Buchanan was sitting on his veranda having an early cup of tea. He watched with interest a lone rider coming down the track towards the homestead. Buchanan noted the well-groomed thoroughbred horse with polished bridle and saddle.

The immaculately dressed rider sat his mount as if he was part of the animal. He also noted how the rider held the reins. He was impressed. Here is a very able rider who may be a very good stockman he thought. The horseman rode up to the edge of the verandah and reined in his mount. After greeting the stranger with a few complimentary remarks about the his horse, he enquired as to his destination. Harry Redford said he was looking for a stockman's job. Without hesitation Nat Buchanan hired him.

After a few days mustering and drafting cattle in various regions of the station, Redford began to work his devious plan moving small mobs of cattle to a far out valley that had good feed. Surely a few hundred cattle from 60,000 would not be missed by the management, he thought. He met three drovers passing through the property on their way further afield. He offered them a well-paid droving job that would last three or four months. The drovers gladly accepted the job. At this point, luck was on Redford's side. The summer rainy season had been very good and he believed good feed for the cattle would be plentiful along the route he had chosen.

Harry Redford's great droving trek now began. They would follow the Thompson River until it met the Barcoo River. These two rivers then ran into Cooper Creek. That must be the only place in the world where two rivers make a creek. Following to a point where the Cooper Creek overflows to form the Strzelecki Creek, this mob of over 1000 head of cattle continued along Strzelecki Creek, resting awhile at Caroowinnie Waterhole and Montecollina Artesian Overflow. The mob of cattle then created the mystifying dust cloud that so intrigued the stockmen at Blanchewater station's Mt

Hopeless outstation.

About this time Nat Buchanan was riding his horse far out from the station homestead looking for well-grassed valleys to shift some of his cattle for the winter months. His sharp eyes noted the trampled grass and many cattle tracks. He ascertained to his surprise that the cattle were running, which appeared strange in such a well-grassed valley.

Suddenly he reined in his horse as he searched the ground and could plainly see shod horse tracks. I've not sent anyone in this region to move cattle, he thought. He shook his reins and urged his horse into a gallop back to the homestead.

"Now I know what happened to that new stockman I engaged a few weeks ago. He disappeared suddenly. That bloke has stolen some of my cattle."

The Queensland mounted police rode out with Nat Buchanan to the point where he had seen the running cattle tracks. The tracks were still very visible. The police then began one of the longest chases to arrest criminals in the history of crime in Australia. They followed the tracks for over 1300 kilometres down the Thompson River and continued along the Barcoo River to the junction with the Cooper Creek. They followed Cooper Creek about one hundred kilometres south until the creek took a sharp turn to the west. At this point the police realised they were near the old Burke and Wills stockade. The police had in their possession maps from Burke and Wills and also Howitt. Suddenly the police stopped in their tracks. Just a few hundred metres ahead a large mob of cattle were grazing along the creek bank. The police immediately believed they had caught up to the cattle thieves. In the distance came the sound of an axe chopping wood. Cautiously the police advanced with guns drawn and called out to two men to stand still with hands above their head. The two men, in total shock at the unexpected appearance of the police, obeyed the instruction. A few moments later Ted Conrick was introducing himself and his assistant to the police. Just a few weeks ago he had arrived from Melbourne with a few sheep and cattle to take up the land he had been granted, Conrick explained. He called his station Nappa Merrie. When Conrick learnt of the police mission he told them that on his arrival he was surprised to see cattle tracks that he believed had passed through that country several months before. The police camped for company with Conrick and his mate that night. Next morning, they continued on down the creek to where Cooper Creek overflows to form Strzelecki Creek. They then continued on to Blanchwater's Mt Hopeless Creek out-station. There the police interviewed the stockmen and station manager. They spent several days at Blanchwater Station where they retrieved the white bull to use as evidence against the cattle duffers.

They continued along the eastern side of the Flinders Ranges to Wilpena Pound and Adelaide. By now the police knew who they were looking for. They also knew the gambling habits of Harry Redford and the likely gambling houses in which to look for him.

Harry Redford was arrested at Bathurst by the New South Wales police and handed over to the Queensland police to be taken to Roma in Western Queensland for trial.

As has happened before in Australia with the infamous criminal Ned Kelly, the media had built the headline stories of Harry Redford's crime into a Robin Hood-type of adventure instead of a crime. Because of the hero's reputation bestowed on Harry Redford by the media, the Queensland Government could see that it would be difficult to get a conviction for the crime. Consequently, they selected a judge for the trial from Sydney, New South Wales. By the time the trial was to begin, hundreds of drovers, shearers, stockmen and members of the media flocked to Roma with the intention of supporting their hero, Harry Redford. When the trial began the courthouse was overflowing with supporters, hundreds waiting on the roadway outside where a man standing in the doorway relayed the proceedings.

After several days the final prosecution and defence demands were completed. The trial judge addressed the jury.

"Gentlemen of the jury have you reached a verdict?"

"Yes, your Honour, we the jury find the defendant NOT GUILTY."

The judge banged on his bench, trying to bring order to the court. He then addressed the jury, "Gentlemen of the jury. Thank God that is your verdict and not mine."

The people of Roma erupted cheering, dancing on the roadway, some even shot their six guns in the air to celebrate the acquittal of their hero. Harry Redford was carried from the courthouse shoulder-high to the cheering of the crowd. A few days later found Harry Redford once again mounted on his beautiful thoroughbred horse and began riding along the Castlereagh Track heading for the Northern Territory. He had to pass through the Western parts of Bowen Downs station and once again he viewed the well-bred cattle grazing on the hillside.

Harry Redford's face held a broad smile as he thought of Nat Buchanan.

He could not resist the temptation of once again lifting several hundred cattle from Nat Buchanan's mob on Bowen Downs. Travelling west droving his newly acquired cattle, he stopped on the vast plains of the Barkley Tablelands in the Northern Territory, set up his own station and called it Brunette Downs.

The development of a station in the remote Northern Territory required more money than Harry Redford could borrow or steal. He accepted a partnership with a Melbourne finance company McAnsh Estates.

After years of hard work and some good and bad years of cattle prices, Harry Redford transformed Brunette Downs into the finest cattle station in Australia. One day he was sitting on the big wide verandah of his large homestead, a bottle of whisky in his hand when he noticed a rider coming down the track towards the homestead. As the stranger got closer he wondered who and why this person was visiting Brunette Downs so far off the beaten track. Surely he would not be looking for station work. Already he had decided the stranger was unemployable as a stockman. He noted the way the rider sat like a bag of potatoes on his shaggy horse. The rider stopped near Harry Redford. He was a young lad of about 18 years.

"Mr Redford," he said, "I've ridden all the way from New South Wales looking for work but no one will give me a start because I am not experienced in station work. Will you give me a start?"

Harry Redford felt for the lad and said, "What is your name?"

The lad answered "Jimmy Miller, sir."

"Son, if you have ridden all the way from New South

Wales looking for work you must be keen enough. I'll tell you what I'll do. If you give me a fair day's work for a fair day's pay, I'll teach you all there is to know about stock-work, cattle management and caring for horses. I'll teach you everything there is to know about running a great cattle station like Brunette Downs."

"Mr Redford I promise you I'll do as you say." Several years later Harry Redford felt quite proud of Jimmy Miller when he was appointed to manage a very large cattle station in the Northern Territory.

As years went by Harry Redford gambled a lot with the sale price of cattle and had lost the confidence of his partners because of their financial position through long periods of low cattle prices. In the end he lost the ownership of Brunette Downs Station. He was broke.

Riding a short distance to the north he took up land and started Anthony Lagoon Station. Years later he lost the ownership of that station. However other station owners knew of his abilities and vast experience. The Amos Brothers, owners of McArthur River station, appointed him to resurrect their station that had been badly managed and lost money. Harry Redford brought that cattle station back to profitability. However as time went by bad cattle prices once again forced McArthur River station deep into debt. The Amos brothers came up from Melbourne and blamed Harry Redford for the financial position that their station was in. They sacked him.

Now an old man in his late seventies Harry Redford considered he was too old to start again. *What should he do now?* he thought as he rode away with his swag strapped to his saddle, that was all he owned in the world. As he rode south he entered his old stamping ground of Brunette Downs that he had developed from nothing to be the greatest cattle station in the country. Oh yes, wasn't that young Jimmy Miller, the lad I had taught all those years ago how to manage a large cattle station.

Jimmy Miller was now the owner of Brunette Downs station and one of the cattle kings of the industry in Australia. He thought maybe he could help Jimmy by working in the saddler's shed to repair and counter-line some of his saddles, plait some girth straps, reins and stock whips. He could do all the leatherwork for the station.

As Harry Redford rode towards the large station homestead he could see Jimmy Miller sitting in his old rocking chair on the verandah. He rode right up to the house and looked into Jimmy Miller's eyes and said, "Jimmy Miller, when you were a lad and arrived here from New South Wales you couldn't get work because you were inexperienced. Remember that? I said to you, *If you give me a fair day's work for a fair day's pay I'll teach you all there is to know about running a great cattle station.*

You kept your word and worked well. I in turn taught you all you know about managing a great cattle station like Brunette Downs. Now as an old man I ask you to return that favour and give me a job as a saddler."

Jimmy Miller stood up from his chair. He pushed his big black hat to the back of his head. Looked up at the wide blue sky above. He returned his eyes to Harry Redford and said,

"Harry Redford, it's a fine day for riding."

In the Territory that always meant. *Get to hell out of here you're not wanted.* Jimmy Miller believed Harry Redford was a gambler and took too many risks with cattle prices and management of the stations. In his eyes Harry Redford was a loser.

With great disappointment and a broken heart Harry Redford turned his horse and rode away from the great cattle station he had established. As he rode he decided to ride over to see his old mate Tom Nugent where he was establishing a new cattle station Banka Banka. He hoped to help Tom Nugent increase his herd by telling him of an acid he knew of that could cloud any brand on a cow's rump. He had used it many times. After all, it was only 500 kilometres across unexplored country to Banka Banka. He had a good horse and vast distances didn't worry an old stager like Harry Redford.

The next day he approached Corella creek and found it in flood with rushing water. However a flooded creek didn't worry him. He plunged his horse into that flooding torrent of water and a floating tree trunk knocked him from his horse and he drowned. A few weeks later when the flooded creek was down, an old Aboriginal woman found the body of Harry Redford and buried him in his swag on the banks of Corella Creek.

Stockmen from Brunette Downs rode out to his grave and placed a simple inscription on a post. Harry Redford BRUNETTE DOWNS.

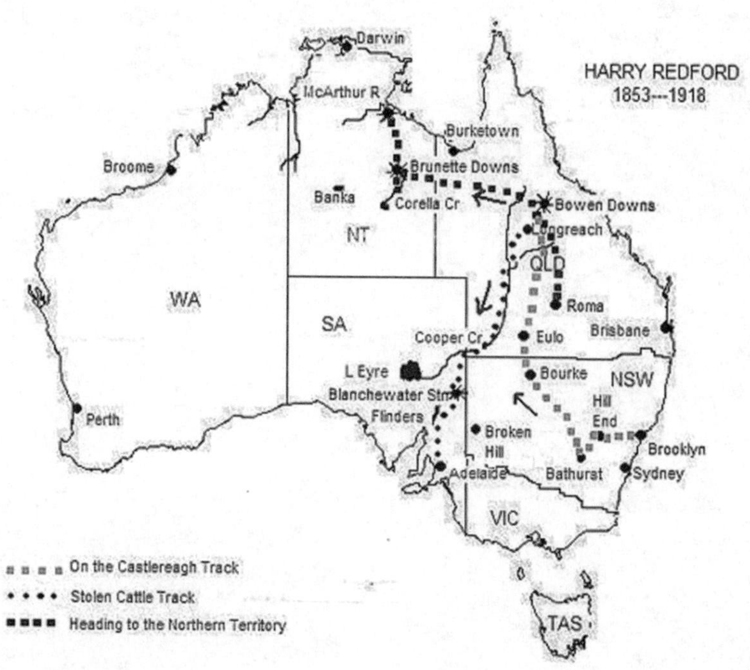

# *Burke and Wills*

On 11th February 1861, four exhausted explorers stopped on a slight rise on a riverbank to make camp for the night. They unloaded their camels and only horse and one of the men strolled down to the creek with a billycan to get water to make a pannikin of tea. Another of the group gathered wood and lit a fire to prepare the evening meal. After the meal, the leader of the group sipped from his pannikin and immediately spat it out.

"Gray, what in the hell did you put in this tea? It tastes awful!"

"Only tea, sir," Gray replied as he took a drink from his own cup of tea. "You are right, sir, it does taste funny. It tastes salty."

At that moment the four men sprang to their feet. They realised that they had just completed the first crossing of the continent of Australia from south to north.

Robert O'Hara Burke arrived in Melbourne in 1853. He was born in Galway, Ireland and as a young man he had experienced some time in the army as well as the Irish police force. Ireland at that time was in famine, many people were starving, because their potato crops had failed. Great stories were appearing in the daily papers of much gold being found in far off Australia. He resigned his job and set sail for Melbourne. On arrival he was advised by locals not to join the thousands of diggers, as most never found any gold.

Instead he joined the Victorian Police force as an acting inspector. In 1858 Burke was appointed to the important position in charge of the Castlemaine Police station. It was here that he saw the headlines in the *Age* newspaper: the first person to cross the continent from south to north would be awarded 3000 pounds. The Government of the colony of South Australia already had a party in the field attempting to complete the journey. The reward was to win a contract to build the new telephone line across Australia, to connect with the undersea cable coming ashore at Darwin from England.

Aafter reading the article Burke wondered if this was his big opportunity for a life much more exciting than a policeman in the country. An adventure like that could make him a hero explorer all over Australia. He would then certainly be in a position to impress Julia Mathews, the famous opera singer he was courting. Burke applied for the position and to the surprise of all, won the position of leader of the Victorian Exploration Expedition. The second-in-command appointment went to Mr George Landells, a camel expert. He was sent to India to purchase 24 camels for the Victorian expedition. He returned with the camels, and also an ex-British soldier, John King, and three sepoys to tend the camels.

Two of the camels were selected as heavy burden carriers, and several others as special riding camels.

Third in command was a young surveyor and astrologist John Wills, 26 years of age. Wills had arrived in Melbourne from Devon with his older brother. His father was a surgeon. At the age of 18, Wills had attended university in England to study medicine and also become a surgeon. However, he changed his mind and came to Australia. The brothers arrived in Melbourne in 1852, followed by their father eight months later. The three headed for the goldfields at Ballarat. Doctor William Wills, physician and surgeon, advertised on a brass plate placed outside his tent. Young John Wills opened a gold buying office next door. He closed that office 12 months later and obtained a position assisting the Professor at the Magnetic Observatory of Melbourne.

Two more scientists were selected. Herman Beckler

as medical officer and botanist and Ludwig Becker as artist, naturalist and geologist. However the only true scientist was John Wills.

Five workmen were engaged including King, Brahe, McDonagh, Gray and Paton.

During the next few months Burke, Landells and Wills were busy gathering and storing supplies and equipment, and training the camels.

On 20th August 1860, the team was ready to begin their great adventure into the unknown.

Burke had last minute meetings with top Government officials, and received his final instructions. He would take the same route as Captain Charles Sturt, 15 years before. He was to travel via Menindee to Cooper Creek to set up his main depot before continuing on to the Gulf of Carpentaria.

The Melbourne newspapers had reported the departure of this great expedition in glowing terms. Thousands of people lined the route out from the Melbourne town hall, waving flags, cheering, and clapping as Robert O'Hara Burke, mounted on his white horse, led the large team of wagons heavily loaded with supplies. Men riding horses and camels made their way from the city and through the districts beyond the outer suburbs. This was the largest team ever assembled for an expedition in Australia. They passed the towns of Kilmore, Bendigo, Kerang and Swan Hill. Between Swan Hill and the crossing of the Murray River at Tooleybuc the country was very boggy and with the heavy wagons continually becoming stuck the expedition lost a lot of time. When they arrived at Balranald they were weeks behind schedule. Burke was now heading northwest, making for Kinchega sheep station near Menindee. By the time they got to the Darling River, Burke and his second in command Landells were arguing continually. When they arrived at Kinchega station, Landells abused Burke in the presence of Mr Wright, the station manager. At this point Burke accepted Landell's resignation. Mr Beckler, the surgeon, also resigned in sympathy with Landells. At this point Burke had lost his second-in-command, the camel expert, and his surgeon. John Wills was now appointed second-in-command. The station manager Mr Wright advised Burke that he needed an experienced bushman for the country ahead. Mr Burke then offered Wright the position as third-in-command and Wright accepted the position.

Because of the very slow progress of this large team, Burke decided to push ahead with just a small number of men, horses and camels.

Burke selected Wills, King, Gray, Brahe, McDonagh, Paton and Mr Wright. The rest of the group with the wagons and supplies would follow at a much slower pace. More bad events were to come when the naturalist Becker also resigned. Burke departed from Menindee heading for Cooper Creek, still hundreds of kilometres to the northwest. Burke left instructions for the rest of his team to follow on to Cooper Creek as fast as possible. It had been a very wet season and much of the country was so boggy that it was very tough going for the horses and camels. Fortunately, the country was well grassed with plenty of feed for the animals. They reached a point near Kokriega and camped in a very large cave for the night. Burke marked this cave *BXXXVI* this being the 36th camp since leaving Melbourne.

Mr Wills kept careful diaries and made close scientific observations about the country they passed through.

Ten days after leaving Menindee, they arrived at Torowoto swamp near the Queensland border. Mr Wright suggested to Burke that it would be a good idea if he went back to make certain the others with the wagons and supplies were coming on. Burke agreed and Wright departed to rejoin the following group. The truth of the matter was that Wright had never been so far into the wilderness, and he became frightened of what lay ahead. Wright returned to Menindee and made no effort to set the others on their way north. One day a trooper mounted on a horse galloped into Menindee with an urgent message for Mr Burke from the Victorian Government. He had been instructed to give that message to nobody else but Burke.

Wright then ordered the trooper to go north on the

tracks left by Burke and he should catch him up in a few days. The trooper was accompanied by a native black-tracker from Kinchega station.

However a week later, the blacktracker returned to report to Wright that the trooper's horse was dead, and that he had left the trooper there with his dead horse to await rescue. Surgeon Beckler went to the rescue with a sepoy and several camels. He returned with the trooper a few days later. Wright learnt that the urgent message was to inform Burke that the rival party of McDouall Stuart from Adelaide, attempting to win the race to the north coast, had been attacked by wild natives and were forced to return to Adelaide. That being the case, there now was no desperate hurry to reach the north coast.

On 11th November, Burke's party arrived at Cooper Creek. They were greeted by thousands of screeching corellas and a beautiful flowing watercourse shaded by hundreds of Red River gums and Coolabah trees. It was a delightful place to establish a main depot.

Burke organised his men to start work building brush store sheds and yards for the horses and camels. Wills, with two camels, set out to explore the country to the north, on the intended route.

He was mainly looking for possible waterholes. However things went terribly wrong with Wills' adventure. His camels escaped and he was forced to return to base on foot, walking more than 160 kilometres, much of the way without food or water. Writing in his diary of this incident Wills said, "There is nothing like a walk of this sort to make you appreciate a drink of water." The temperature that day was 40°C.

Burke was expecting Wright with the wagons and supplies at anytime. He was very unhappy with the delay and was impatient to continue his journey. When there was no sign of Wright and the rest of the group, Burke made his momentous decision to once again divide his group. His plan was to go on to the gulf with Wills, King, and Gray, leaving Brahe, McDonagh and Paton at Cooper Creek depot to wait for the group commanded by Wright. Burke would take the horse he would ride, and three camels carrying light rations to last 3 months.

"I am leaving you in charge Brahe," Burke said, "until Mr Wright arrives with the others and the supplies. We ought to be back, I calculate inside 3 months. You must tell Mr Wright positively that we are taking only enough food for 13 weeks, and that we expect to return with little food to spare. Whatever happens, Mr Wright must leave sufficient food here for us, if he finds it is necessary to return to Menindee. Tell Mr Wright that we are making our way along Eyre Creek. I trust you absolutely Brahe. Do you understand what I am saying?"

"Yes, sir," Brahe replied. "I understand and I will do as you ask."

"There is one more thing I wish to say. This is a

private instruction to you personally. We never know what may happen on an expedition such as this. I have certain personal papers that I do not wish to lose. Also I do not want them to fall into any other person's hands. I will trust you Brahe to do as I ask. Throw them into the river if I do not return," Burke instructed.

"I promise, sir," replied Brahe.

The leader unlocked a tin box and took from it a small parcel and red sealing wax. Burke lit a taper and Brahe watched silently as his leader affixed heavy seals to the package, pressing his signet ring into the wax. Burke shook hands with Brahe and bade him good night.

On Sunday morning 16th December, Wills wrote in his field book, "The horse and camels are ready. We start out at 6am tomorrow."

By the 19th December the four men were well on their way into the trackless stony desert. The expedition was now split into three parts. The leader Burke and his group were well on the way to Eyre Creek. Brahe and the two other men were at Cooper Creek building Fort Wills stockade and the rearguard commanded by Wright was still in a state of inactivity back at Menindee.

Burke and his companions travelled on. Christmas Day saw them jolting along on their camels in the morning until they stopped at a flowing creek. Burke was anxious to push on but one of their camels lay down in the shade of a big coolabah tree and refused to move. From

Boxing Day they continued on for five days along this creek. Diary entries became very scrappy from this point onwards. They obviously were straining every nerve in their bodies to reach their objective. Descending the Selwyn Ranges, which Burke named, they came to the headwaters of the Cloncurry River, also named by Burke. They were now well into the tropics. One day Wills told Burke that they had just passed a reference on the map indicating where the explorer Leichhardt had passed, on his journey to the Northern Territory a few years before.

One night they camped on the banks of a fine river. Burke made a little speech about a lady friend back in Melbourne. He then named the river Julia Creek after Julia Mathews, a famous opera singer.

After crossing the creek the next morning they continued on until January 30th. On that day one of their camels became bogged and they had to abandon the animal.

In the meantime, back at Cooper Creek, Brahe and his men had cut timber and built a stockade eight metres square. The men had a relaxing Christmas day still waiting for Wright to arrive from the south.

Weeks passed and still Wright had not arrived. Early in February Burke was preparing for his last push in his attempt to reach the Gulf of Carpentaria. After a hard day's travel in hot conditions the four exhausted explorers stopped to make camp for the night on a slight rise on the bank of a flowing creek.

Both Burke and Wills sat writing in their diaries. After their evening meal was eaten, Burke sipped from his pannikin of tea and growled. "Gray, what did you put in this tea? It tastes funny."

"Only tea, sir," he said as he took a drink from his pannikin.

"You are right sir. It does taste funny. It tastes salty," said Gray. At that moment the four men jumped to their feet with astonishment.

"Salty!" shouted Wills.

"Tidal waters!" cried Burke. "We have reached the Gulf!" They all rushed down the bank and tasted the water. It was salty sailor Gray who shouted enthusiastically, "It's sea water, make no mistake about that. I know the smell of sea water."

Wills remarked, "Those small trees are mangrove trees."

"Success at last," Burke remarked. "Only another mile or two and we've crossed the continent."

That night they had broken sleep, pestered by mosquitoes and lying on wet mangrove leaves. In the morning Burke instructed King and Gray to remain in camp. Burke suggested that he and Wills would attempt to reach the seashore. They took the horse and set off through the mangrove swamp. However the horse had great difficulty in the muddy conditions and continually got bogged. Burke decided to tie his horse to a tree and then continue through the mud with Wills. Now they knew it was in fact tidal, as the water rising made it impossible for the men to advance. Huge crocodiles threatened, lurking near the struggling men in chest-deep water. Still they had not reached the seashore. They even climbed trees in a desperate attempt to see the open sea without success. Burke and Wills returned to retrieve the horse and disappointed, arrived back at their camp.

After resting that day and night, Burke said, "King, get ready to travel tomorrow. We begin our return journey in the morning."

The 1100 kilometre journey from Cooper Creek that had started on 16th December 1860 had taken till the 11th February 1861 – 8 weeks. As they had started with food for only three months, the problem now was how to return to Cooper Creek with only enough rations to last them five weeks.

Wills' mathematical precision planned the daily allowance for the return journey. Each man would be rationed to less than half a kilogram of flour and ten sticks of dried meat. This was to be supplemented with any native animals or birds along with yams. On these rations the return journey began. The men were now in good spirits as they looked forward to their return to base.

The tropical storms, complete with lightning, thunder and heavy rain, hindered their progress. The ground was now very boggy, and the horse and camels had great difficulty as they floundered through the mud. On 25th February they travelled in the moonlight to take advantage of some harder ground and cooler conditions. The days were now extremely hot and humid. When the weather cleared they made much better progress.

A grand reunion took place when they came across the camel that had laid in the shade on the banks of Eyre creek and had refused to continue on the outward journey. On that occasion they abandoned the camel and it remained in the area and appeared happy to rejoin the other camels.

The next day King caught a large python snake and decided to make a snake stew. However this proved to be unwise as Burke fell ill and was unable to keep his seat on his camel the next day. Gray also complained of very bad headaches and gradually got worse and was unable to assist in any way. The four men struggled on and on, kilometre after kilometre. The camels were also showing signs of distress; their once fat humps were now as flat as pancakes. Burke's horse was very scraggy and weak. The explorers were also showing terrible strain and weakness.

That night Burke spoke seriously to Wills. "My dear boy, how far are we from Cooper Creek?"

"About 480 kilometres," Wills replied.

"We haven't enough food for that period," Burke

suggested. "We will check our gear and reduce as much of it as is practical. Carry only the bare essentials."

They opened their packs and discarded over 30 kilograms weight of clothes and instruments. More rain fell and there came a serious problem when Gray was caught stealing food and was severely cautioned by Burke.

Back at the stockade at Cooper Creek, Brahe expected his leader to return around the 15th March. He had also expected Wright and the wagons with the supplies to appear at the base. On 4th April when Burke and his party were overdue, Brahe became very nervous. He thought Burke's party may have been killed or perished in the desert. Or maybe they had made it to the Gulf and had been picked up by a passing ship.

The next day he told Paton to shoe the horses and prepare for departure soon. However, Paton became sick and Brahe thought he was showing signs of scurvy. This convinced Brahe to depart the stockade and start the return to Menindee. "We will leave here next Sunday, 21st April," he told them.

While Brahe decided to desert the stockade, back at Menindee, Wright had finally started to prepare to travel on to the Cooper Creek stockade. At this time Burke, Wills, King and Gray struggled on, foot sore, ragged and hungry. Only through the determined spirit of their leader did the men continue their agonising progress.

They had on their minds the warm campfire, great meals, a change of clothes and new boots, and the friendly faces of Brahe, Wright and the others welcoming them back. Their progress now had become much slower as Gray had become seriously ill and had to be tied to the camel he was riding to prevent him falling off.

That night as they lay by the fire under the stars Gray crawled over to near Wills and said, "Mr Wills, I think I'm going to die."

Wills replied, "Don't be silly Gray, just think, in a day or two we'll be back at the stockade. You ought to be ashamed of yourself, a big husky sailor like you talking about dying."

Next morning, on the 17th April, Gray was dead. Burke, Wills and King spent the whole day digging a grave with their bare hands. Burke said what he could remember of the service. Whilst they were burying their companion, just 100 kilometres away from Cooper Creek, Brahe had made his final preparations to depart, unknown to Burke whose very life depended on not losing any time.

Brahe buried a small quantity of food in a box beneath a Coolabah tree, and blazed the tree with the words. "DIG 3 feet down at 40 feet NW". Brahe kept most of the food for his party's return to Menindee. Brahe then called McDonagh aside and said, "I want you to witness something."

He unstrapped a camel trunk and withdrew a small sealed package, then explained to McDonagh that Mr Burke wished his private papers to be destroyed if he failed to return.

"If Mr Burke is not dead he'll be pretty wild with you," McDonagh said.

"Oh, he's dead alright," Brahe said. "If the blacks haven't killed him, he may have gone the same way as Doctor Leichhardt and starved to death."

The unopened package was thrown into the campfire and burnt. On April 21st, at sunset, Brahe and the others were 20 kilometres away from Cooper Creek. At the time of the same sunset, in their last stage of exhaustion, Burke, Wills and King decided that as they were now so close to the Cooper Creek stockade that they would continue on. Wills told Burke he believed they were only 16 kilometres away. As the stockade came in sight Burke said he could smell the stew cooking on the campfire.

Burke called out, "Brahe, McDonagh Paton, we made it to the Gulf we are back." But there was only silence. No smell of stews cooking on the fire. Wills in desperation called. "Is there anybody here?" There was only the croaking of frogs in the nearby creek.

Burke sank to his knees in despair, too overcome to speak.

Wills croaked, "King, they have gone?"

The three men sat dejected with their chins sunk on their chest. Wills painfully stood up and walked out of the stockade and down to the river to get a bucket of water. King began to light a fire. Suddenly Wills paused. He saw that a tree had recently been blazed. He staggered across to see the meaning of it. With the scent of the newly blazed tree fresh in his nostrils he stared at the inscription, "DIG 3 feet down at 40 feet NW."

"Mr Burke come here and have a look at this." Wills called out. Burke staggered over and stood next to Wills.

"DIG." he repeated. The two men stood in silence a moment. Wills said, "Those words were cut this very day."

King called, "There is a new mark on the tree."

The men stared at the date. APRIL 21.

"That is the date today," said Wills.

"Dig, dig," Burke ordered. "See what message they have left." King dug about 3 feet down in the newly disturbed earth and uncovered a small box. Opening the box, Wills took out a message and handed to Burke as he said, "So they have really gone." Again the message had the same date of departure.

Wills busied himself making some flour cakes from the small packet of food Brahe had left buried under the coolabah tree. Burke clutched the message left by Brahe that explained that Mr Wright had not arrived with wagons and supplies, so he reluctantly departed from the

Cooper Creek stockade. Brahe's message continued, "I firmly believe Mr Burke and his group will not return. The date of their expected return is long past."

Wills came over to his leader and placing a hand on his shoulder said, "Come and have something to eat, sir."

During the night, Burke considered his party's position. He thought it would be impossible to catch up to Brahe and his men all on well-rested horses. He planned to remain at the stockade two days. Then with their three remaining camels to proceed down river for about 50 kilometres, then make a dash to get across the Cobbler desert to the nearest civilisation, Mt Hopeless station, north of the Flinders Ranges. Before departing, Wills had finalised all his notes and diaries on the expedition. He then placed his papers with a note from Mr Burke telling of his exact plans of the route he was taking in case a relief party arrived. Wills then buried the box in the same hole that Brahe had left the food in, under the tree.

With many glances back they slowly made their way downstream riding their weary camels, in a south-westerly direction. Wills had calculated they had about 20 day's provisions left to reach Mt Hopeless cattle station, 340 kilometres away across the desert. Meanwhile, on the first night that Burke and his party had arrived at the stockade, Brahe, McDonagh and Paton were only 25 kilometres away camped on a creek. The next day they continued eastward, and after another day they could see smoke in the distance that they believed to be a campfire. On arrival near the campfire Brahe was amazed to see that it was Wright and his wagon with the long-awaited supplies. "Where is Mr Burke?" Wright asked.

"I don't know," answered Brahe. "We waited 120 days for him to return and also for you to arrive with supplies."

Offering no excuse for his delay, Wright never-the-less said he had come this far, he wanted to see the stockade at Cooper Creek.

Brahe started back to Cooper Creek with Mr Wright. After several more days the two arrived at the stockade. Sitting on their horses without dismounting, Brahe showed Wright the blaze on the tree and pointed out where he had buried the box of food. They could see that the earth over the buried box had not been disturbed. They did not notice any of the tracks that Burke and Wills had made during the two days they were there. Shortly after the two men rode away without realising Burke, Wills and King had returned to the stockade after their ordeal on the expedition to the Gulf.

Burke, Wills and King soon had more troubles to contend with. Several days after leaving the stockade one of the camels became bogged and they had to shoot it. The next night a second camel died. Now they were in a hopeless position and would not be able to attempt the desert crossing. Their only alternative was to try to return to the stockade and hope for a rescue party.

The practical minded Wills and the optimistic King had studied the way the natives had made flour from nardoo plants seeds. So they began searching for nardoo plants.

They hoped that flour might keep them alive. Burke however disagreed and said, "A man would starve if he relied on that stuff. We are not savages."

It was now winter and the nights were very cold. The three men huddled close together around their campfire.

In the morning Burke was readying himself to start on his long walk up stream towards the stockade. Wills said he would stay behind and search for more nardoo plants, or maybe make friends with the natives who they could see in the distance most days.

Burke replied, "I will have nothing to do with the savages."

Whenever Burke saw any natives in the bush he would fire shots from his revolver over their heads to frighten them away. Wills was always disappointed with the attitude of Burke towards the Aboriginal people. More so at this time when those very people were the only ones that could probably keep the three men alive until rescued.

As Burke and King walked away Wills called out, "I'll catch up to you both tomorrow."

When the two men walked on Wills sat under the very tree he was to die under, probably that night. Burke and King struggled on all day. Burke was by now in a very bad way and King had to assist his leader to walk.

Next morning Burke said he thought that they were still 40 kilometres from the stockade. "I don't think I will make it," he said.

It was near midday, as they staggered along the riverside, Burke collapsed to the ground. He was completely exhausted. King made him as comfortable as possible, leaning him against a large coolabah tree.

"I'm finished," Burke told King.

He lay there for some time, King brought him a drink of water from the river.

"I will not last much longer," Burke said in a slurred voice. "This is my last order to you, King." Burke indicated to King to take his pistol from his pack and place it in his hand. King obeyed his leader's order. As he placed the pistol in Burke's hand a faint smile appeared on Burke's face. Shortly after the pistol slid from Burke's hand. King saw that Burke was dead.

King buried the body of his leader, then set off down the river to look for Wills. He was shocked and saddened to fine Wills dead under the tree where he and Burke had left him several days before.

King was unaware that Aborigines in the bushes were watching him. The friendly natives now recognising that

King was alone, approached him with food and friendship. With the help of the natives King soon regained fitness.

The Aborigines demonstrated to King that plenty of food was available in the Cooper Creek region to the experienced bushman.

Kangaroos and wallabies in the bush, ducks and swamphens on the riverbank. The waters of the Cooper Creek were teaming with large fish and mussels. King thought, *If only Burke had used his rifle and ammunition to provide food instead of shooting over the heads of the natives to frighten them away. Surely they all would have survived.*

Three months later a search party led by Alfred Howitt rescued King. The box of Wills' records that Wills had buried near the Dig Tree was retrieved. Thus the story of the infamous and disastrous Burke and Wills expedition was recorded in the history of Australia.

**Author's note:**
*I have experienced many wonderful days and nights camped at the Dig Tree. It is impossible for me to conceive anyone dying of starvation at that delightful place. Burke must take credit for being the most inept explorer in our history.*

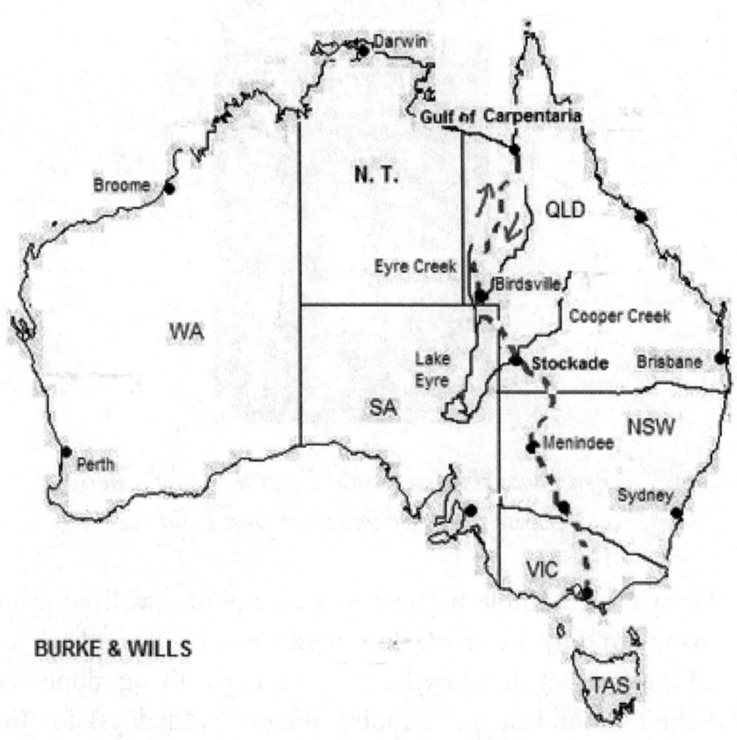
Darwin
Gulf of Carpentaria
N. T.
Broome
QLD
Eyre Creek
Birdsville
Cooper Creek
WA
Lake
Eyre
Stockade
Brisbane
SA
NSW
Menindee
Perth
Sydney
VIC
BURKE & WILLS
TAS

Also by Bert Bolton

# On the Outback Tracks

STORIES FROM AN OUTBACK LEGEND

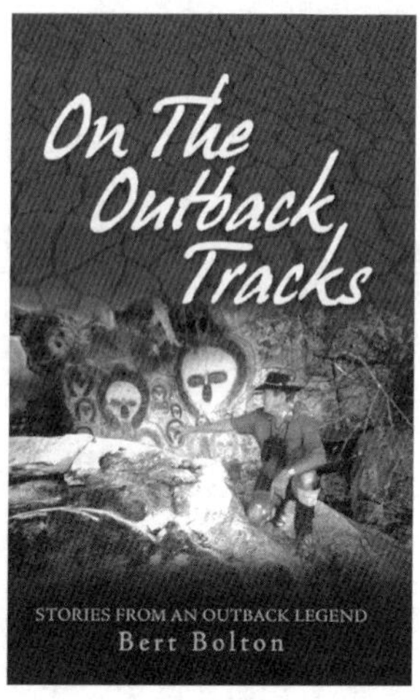


*When I was three-years-old I wanted to be a horse because my horse had shoes and I didn't.*

From these humble beginnings Bert Bolton has lived a life many can only dream of. Born with a love of the outback his adventures begun when he was making a living along the Rabbit Proof Fence – trapping dingos (wild dogs) for the Government in outback Western Australia.

Well known by thousands of Australians who have been on his *Outback Track Tours*, he has been painted by Rolf Harris, taught how to hunt and gather food by local Aboriginies in Arnhem Land, and discovered breath-taking Wandjina art in Kimberley caves. From around a campfire and along a dusty road, these are the stories of a true outback man.

## Order your copy of:

| | | Qty |
|---|---|---|
| Stories of the Outback | RRP AU$29.99 | ..... |
| On the Outback Tracks | RRP AU$29.99 | ..... |
| | Postage within Aust. AU$6.00 | ..... |
| | | ---------- |
| | TOTAL* | $________ |

* All prices include GST

Name: ____________________________________________

Address: ____________________________________________

____________________________________________

Phone: ____________________________________________

Email Address: ____________________________________________

**Method of Payment:**

❑ Money Order ❑ Cheque ❑ Amex ❑ MasterCard ❑ Visa

Cardholder's Name: ____________________________________________

____________________________________________

Credit Card Number: ____________________________________________

Signature: ______________________________ Expiry Date: __________

Allow 21 days for delivery.

**Payment to:**

Better Bookshop (ABN 14 067 257 390)
PO Box 12544
A'Beckett Street, Melbourne, 8006
Victoria, Australia
Fax: +61 3 9671 4730 Email: betterbookshop@brolgapublishing.com.au